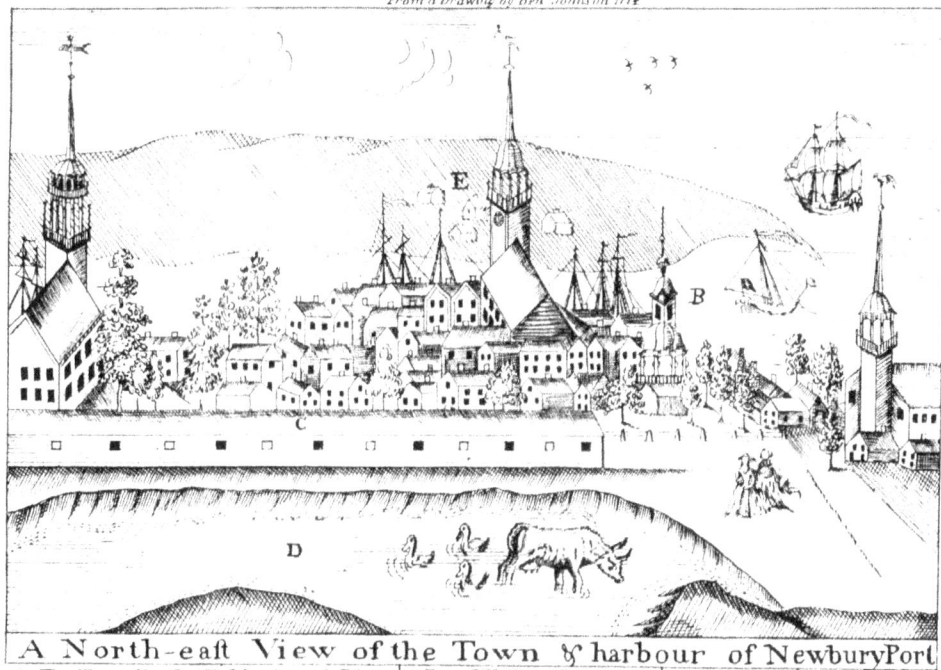

A North-east View of the Town & harbour of NewburyPort

A The Town Houfe | B. Merrimack River | C RopeWalk | D Frog Pond | E. Salifbury

This 1744 engraving by Ben Johnson shows cows grazing on the Frog Pond and active trade on the Merrimack River. *From Currier's* History of Newburyport.

A Brief History of

OLD NEWBURY

From Settlement to Separation

BETHANY GROFF

THE
History
PRESS

Published by The History Press
Charleston, SC 29403
www.historypress.net

First published 2008
Second printing 2009
Third printing 2012
Fourth printing 2012

ISBN 978-1-5402-1880-3

Groff, Bethany.
A brief history of Old Newbury : from settlement to separation / Bethany Groff.
p. cm.
Includes bibliographical references and index.
ISBN 978-1-5402-1880-3
1. Newbury (Mass.)--History--17th century. 2. Newbury
(Mass.)--History--18th century. 3. Newbury (Mass.)--Social conditions. 4.
Newbury (Mass.)--Economic conditions. I. Title.
F74.N53G76 2008
974.4'5--dc22
2008029855

To Emily Noyes Poore, my Aunt Emily.

CONTENTS

PREFACE

My office as regional site manager for the North Shore of Massachusetts for Historic New England looks out on the back end of the house that Daniel Peirce built in 1690, five years before he hunted down a raiding party of Indians to rescue a Newbury family, and a decade before he was given the honor of choosing the first seat in the meetinghouse. It sits on John Spencer's 1635 land grant. The Little family, descendants of one of Newbury's first settlers, George Little, lived here for 135 years, and hundreds of the sons and daughters of Newbury families have worked in its fields, barns and kitchens. I myself am a descendant of John and Mary Emery (twice), Daniel and Sarah Peirce (three times), George and Alice Little (twice) and Tristram and Judith Coffin (a rather embarrassing eight times over), along with a host of other early Newbury couples whose obligation to be fruitful and multiply was taken to heart. The past residents of Newbury are still everywhere, if you're looking for them, in houses, churches, burying grounds and the long memories of those few souls whose families have been here for generations. When I undertook to write this book, I thought that the continuing presence of Newbury's early settlers in my life and my family would somehow uniquely prepare me to write about early Newbury and that much of my work was already done.

Once I began to write, however, I discovered complicated, unique people I had never met before, whose names and dates give no hint of their personalities and proclivities. I came to be very fond of the flirty Mary Rolfe, who was caught in a pleasant seduction, but was afraid for her reputation. Reverend John Woodbridge came off in the record as a haughty and self-important man, whose attempts to serve his community were often met with scorn. I spent many hours scanning the Essex County quarterly court records and finding a record of a man or woman I knew well, speaking in a voice that I had come to recognize. Joshua Coffin, the abolitionist and antiquarian, laid a great deal of groundwork and had access to many vanished sources when he wrote his history of Newbury in 1845. John J. Currier followed fifty years later with two volumes. Both of these authors produced works of immense value to me and did great service to the history of the community. Still, there was much left to find, if only to flesh out the characters or relationships of people identified by Coffin and Currier. There is an extraordinary wealth of information about this place, and I quickly discovered just how much I didn't know.

Tristram Coffin House, built in 1678. His great-great-great-granddaughter Lucy Coffin, seen here on the lawn, was the last person to live in the house. *Private collection.*

In my efforts to rectify that, I must thank first my husband, Adam, whom I met in a graduate history class and who is uniquely suited to understanding my paroxysms of delight upon the discovery of one obscure record or another, and whose many long nights of careful editing shaped this book into its final form; and my children, Jed and Meg, who are patient and kind. Emily Gustainis, the librarian and archivist at Historic New England, proved to me why our collection and staff are among the best in the nation, and Jay Williamson and Nancy Thurlow at the Historical Society of Old Newbury gave generously of their time and knowledge. Dorothy LaFrance, the head librarian at Newburyport Public Library, was kind enough to leave me alone in a conference room with a portrait of the seriously gorgeous Moses Titcomb, and Chris Drelich, whose work on the website www.newbury375.org is a wonderful journey through Newbury images, provided generous support. Dick Cunningham did me the great honor of having the first read-through of a messy manuscript, and Carl Panall's comments on early European explorers were particularly useful. My cousin, Sue Follansbee, and my great-aunt, Louise Muzrall, have been a wellspring of knowledge. Diane Rapaport and Professor Emerson Baker at Salem State College both provided wonderful, pertinent guidance. My staff and co-workers, and the intrepid adventurers of the 1919 SPL Reading Club, have put up with my carrying on about dead people for years. I must also, of course, thank

Rachel Roesler and Saunders Robinson at The History Press, both of whom have been a pleasure to work with and without whom this project would not have been possible. Lastly, Mom and Dad have lived like colonists and prayed like them, too, and for that, and uncountable hours of babysitting, I am deeply indebted.

Please note: I have kept the flavor of early writing whenever possible, but have standardized spelling and punctuation for easier reading. I have also standardized dates using the Gregorian calendar.

CHAPTER 1

To 1635

Pre-Contact and Exploration

There is also Okes, Pines, Walnuts, and other wood to make this place an excellent habitation…
—John Smith, describing Plum Island

Newbury first appears on maps as a curving line of ink, Cape Ann its chin, Plum Island a lozenge before the open mouth of the Merrimack River, a high forehead above stretching to the Piscataqua. It is first identified in the book *New England's Prospect* by William Wood, published in 1634, variously as Quasacunqud, Merrimack and, on the eve of settlement, Wessacucon. Though the Englishmen who landed in the early spring of 1635 would find what seemed to be a virgin landscape, glaciers and the sea had shaped Newbury for thousands of years.

Before human hands cut, burned, planted and reaped along its fertile coast and forest, receding sheets of ice stranded massive boulders in strange places and piled debris into drumlins of one hundred to two hundred feet, most notably in the form of Old Town Hill. As the glaciers melted and sea levels rose, coastal plains flooded and deposited sediment to the tops of high dunes, forming Plum Island. Between the sea and the land, salt-tolerant grasses spread and, as they died, formed a thick layer of peat marsh. Leftover sand and rock formed numerous small islands, later a welcome refuge for farmers when the land disappeared at high tide. Up a slow rise, salt marsh yielded to bayberries, blueberries and plums, then to forests of hickory, oak and chestnut.

There is no record of how the first humans found Newbury, but when they arrived around ten thousand years ago, they hunted, gathered, fished and made little impact on the land. They left behind bits of chipped stone weaponry and little else. It was not until Algonquin peoples settled in Newbury some two thousand years ago that humans left a mark. By 1634, the area that would later be downtown Newburyport is identified as Pentucket; perhaps an Indian village or perhaps a trading station that belonged to John Winthrop Jr., of Agawam (today Ipswich), who in 1633 was given permission "to set up a trucking House up Merrimack River."

The Agawam groups that lived in Newbury were Pennacook (meaning "at the bottom of the hill or highland"), a confederation of tribes of the Algonquin linguistic group. The only chief, or sagamore, of the Agawam tribe with whom the Europeans had contact was Masconomet, who seems to have been initially glad of the European presence in

Ipswich and Newbury, as it offered his decimated tribe some protection from the warlike bands to the North. The Agawam were a seasonally agricultural group. They settled on the most fertile ground along rivers and cleared fields of trees using the bark-stripping girdling technique. They planted corn and beans and squash among the stumps, an important supplement to the berries and seeds they gathered and the meat they hunted. Burning out the underbrush in forests created a perfect habitat for deer and other game animals and made hunting them far easier.

Pennacook villages were mobile units, though there were traditional meeting places, often linked to religious ritual, that were consistent for generations. Lodges made from a wood frame covered with hide sheltered several family groups, and villages remained in place as long as the ground was fertile and the hunting and fishing sufficient. Though these groups moved seasonally from one area to another, they had distinct regional areas of control. The Agawam group whose village site gave way to the first Newbury settlement had spent centuries clamming along Joppa Flats, picking berries and beach plums on Plum Island and hunting deer through the tall forests of Byfield. They had set their weirs at the Parker River falls, gone out from Deer and Carr Island to catch sea bass and eels using lobster as bait, and trapped sturgeon and salmon, which, mixed with ground corn, was their staple food. Daniel Gookin, superintendent of the Indians around Boston, was moved to remark in 1674:

> *I have wondered many times that they were not in danger of being choked with fish bones; but they are so dexterous in separating the bones from the fish in their eating thereof that they are in no hazard.*[1]

Deer, bear, otter and raccoon were dried and added to the pottage along with the fish. Small portable cakes, called *nokake*, were made of ground corn and flavored with wild herbs, picked in the forests and fields that the first English settlers found empty in 1635.

Though the first group of English men, women and children who stepped off their shallop in the early spring of 1635 must have felt like they were the first Europeans to encounter the place (they were well aware of a potentially menacing native presence), they were relative latecomers in the exploration of the Merrimack River and Plum Island. In fact, the previous comings and goings of dozens of traders, trappers, fishermen and adventurers had virtually ensured that they would not find the natives hostile. In fact, they would find hardly any natives at all.

Early in the morning of July 16, 1605, the French explorer Samuel de Champlain and several members of his crew made land on the eastern tip of Cape Ann. Champlain, accompanied by his patron, the wealthy Pierre De Monts, had spent a harsh winter on an island in the St. Croix river between Maine and New Brunswick and was eager to move southward. Champlain had a generally positive relationship with the natives he encountered; so much so that on his way south, he stopped to ask for directions. Specifically, he asked a group of native men he encountered to look over the map of the coast he had drawn and add notable features. The native men

View from Old Town Hill. *Courtesy of the Historical Society of Old Newbury.*

added the outline of Massachusetts Bay, and also drew in the mouth of the Merrimack River. It is also possible that at this time, Europeans first heard the name of that great river, called in the earliest records Merimacke, Merimack, Merrimacke, Merrimake and Merrymake.

Nine years later, Captain John Smith, of Jamestown, Virginia fame, left most of his men on Monhegan Island off the coast of Maine, busily drying and salting codfish, and set off with eight others to explore the southerly coast and trade for fur. He made a careful study of the numerous inlets, islands and harbors that he encountered from Monhegan Island to Cape Cod, and he published an account of his travels, along with a detailed map, the following year in London. Smith named bits of the coast as he went, from Cape Ann to Smith's Isles (now the Isles of Shoals, off the New Hampshire coast). He named the whole region "New England," and it so pleased Charles, Prince of Wales, that Smith proudly announced to his supporters back home that the prince "was pleased to confirm it by that title." Smith does not appear to have left names for the coast and islands that would later become Newbury, but he did leave the first detailed description of Plum Island:

> *On the east an isle of two or three leagues in length the one half plain marsh ground, fit for pasture or salt ponds, with many fair high groves of mulberry trees and gardens; there is also oaks, pines, walnuts and other wood to make this place an excellent habitation being a good and safe harbor.*[2]

In 1622, Captain John Mason, former governor of Newfoundland, was granted

> *all the lands lying along the Atlantic from Naumkeag River to the Merrimack River and extending back to the heads of these rivers…together with the Great Isle or Island henceforth to be called Isle Mason lying near or before the bay, harbor of the River Agawam.*

So it seems that the first name for Plum Island was Isle Mason, but not for long. Though the lands that made up the Mason grant were unsettled in 1622, they would soon be swarming with Europeans with various claims on the land, and it appears that Plum Island was seldom, if ever, referred to as Isle Mason after 1635.

It was the enigmatic "Great Watt," however, who provided a glimpse of how the first European explorers encountered Newbury. Before settlers began to arrive by the boatload, the New England coast and the mouth of the Merrimack had been traversed many times by European traders and fishermen, hauling huge cod out of the Atlantic, salting and drying them, much as Captain Smith's men were doing on Monhegan Island, and shipping them back to Europe. The shores of the Merrimack River were sprinkled with cod flakes, platforms used to ensure even drying of the split, salted fish. Sturgeon and salmon also crowded the Merrimack River, and though they were never caught in such quantity as cod, they were also a ready source of income when pickled and shipped back to Europe in barrels.

"Watt's Cellar" appears repeatedly on the very earliest deeds in Newbury, along with the path that led to it, called "the way to Watt's Cellar," now State Street. The cellar itself seems to have been part of some sort of storage building, perhaps built partly into the bank, and was located near where the Firehouse stands today, opposite Market Square. A man named Walter Bagnall appears in an entry in John Smith's journal dated October 22, 1631, identified as "Great Watt," a fur trader with a reputation for dishonesty. Walter Bagnall was a companion of Thomas Morton, who had defied the Puritan government and sent up a distinctly un-Puritan town at Mare Mount (now Quincy). Bagnall went north after Morton was arrested by Plymouth Colony officials, and it is likely that Watt's Cellar belonged to him. In 1631, he made a fateful move to Maine, where he was murdered. Smith's diary records the event, and the first settlers of Newbury would likely have heard about it when they arrived in 1635.

> *The governor* [John Winthrop] *received a letter from Capt. Wiggin of Pascataquack* [Portsmouth, New Hampshire], *informing him of a murder committed the third of this month at Richman's Isle* [Richmond Island, off Cape Elizabeth, Maine], *by an Indian sagamore, called Squidrayset, and his company, upon one Walter Bagnall, called Great Watt, and one John P———, who kept with him. They, having killed them, burnt the house over them, and carried away their guns and what else they liked…This Bagnall…was a wicked fellow, and had much wronged the Indians.*[3]

Extensive archeological exploration in the 1970s turned up fascinating bits of early pottery and building materials, but where and what the cellar was, we may never know. The Great Watt and his cellar remain an enduring Newbury mystery.

Deed to a portion of Newbury (later Byfield), purchased by Henry Sewell in 1681 from the descendants of "Old Will Indian." *Perley's* Indian Land Titles of Essex County.

It was men like Watt, Smith and Champlain whose early contact with native peoples provided invaluable information to potential settlers—and also ensured that the land between the Parker and Merrimack Rivers would be largely uninhabited when those settlers arrived. Though exact numbers are very difficult to obtain, it has been estimated that there were over ten thousand Pennacook in the Merrimack Valley when first contact was made with European fishermen and traders in the late sixteenth century. By 1620, however, chickenpox, measles and various other common European diseases to which the native peoples had no immunity had reduced their number to just over a thousand. Many villages were wiped out entirely. For other communities, it was a time of shifting allegiance and great uncertainty as bands reformed from the remnants of devastated families.

There are scattered references to native peoples in Newbury in some early documents; two deeds still in existence and one recorded from the original imply that some thought was given to native ownership of Newbury land. But what native presence remained in the area offered no resistance to the first settlers. It was not until sixty-five years after settlement that the sons of the first settlers would find it necessary to pay for the land, and by then it was the ironically named Samuel English, the grandson and heir of Masconomet, the sagamore of Agawam, whose squiggled mark signifies the release of all lands to the English on January 10, 1700.

By then, among the Newbury residents, the ten thousand acres paid for and witnessed before justices of the peace Daniel Peirce and Thomas Noyes had been bought, sold, built on, cleared and planted many times over. This grandson of Masconomet released all rights to the town for the sum of ten pounds. The deed makes the English claim on the natural world complete and leaves no room for ambiguity: Samuel English releases "all the wood, timber, lands, grounds, soils, waters, streams, rivers, ponds, huntings, stones, mines, [and] minerals" within the bounds of Newbury. Later, in January, the same Samuel English pressed his claim on the town of Rowley, which then included parts of present-day Byfield, and was paid nine pounds, to be raised by the townsfolk.

CHAPTER 2

ARRIVAL

First Settlement, 1635

This Country Hath Not that Which this Place cannot Yield.
—William Wood, 1634, describing the land on the banks of the Merrimack River

Before 1630, land in the New World was mainly granted to individuals or private companies. Often the boundaries of these lands overlapped, and it was difficult to mediate disputed grants from England. As English settlers began to arrive by the hundreds, and then the thousands, it was decided that control of the affairs of the Massachusetts Bay Colony would be transferred to a "Great and General Court." The first General Court met in Charlestown in 1630, and its members agreed to forbid anyone to settle within the colony without first gaining the permission of the governor and the General Court. A warrant was issued to remove those who had already illegally settled at Agawam (later Ipswich). In 1633, the Court ordered that "a plantation should be begun at Agawam, being the best in the land for tillage and cattle, lest an enemy, finding it void, should possess it and take it from us." The following March, a group of twelve men settled in Agawam, among them George Carr, who later operated the ferry system between Newbury and Salisbury and for whom Carr's Island (more commonly Carr Island today), in the mouth of the Merrimack, is named.

In 1634, William Wood published *New England's Prospect*, which sought to provide prospective colonists with a description of what they would find here. Wood described Agawam as being

> the best place but one, which is Merrimack…All along the river side is fresh marshes, in some places three miles broad. In this river is sturgeon, salmon, and bass, and diverse other kinds of fish…There are scarce any inhabitants in these two places.

Wood also refers briefly to the fishermen, who were already well acquainted with Newbury. "The best catching of them (sturgeon) be…in the river Merrimack where much is taken, pickled, and brought for England, some of them be 12, 14, 18 foot long." It is in this book that the first map showing Plum Island, the Merrimack River and the Quasacunqud (later Parker) River appears.

New England's Prospect had its desired effect in England, and as settlers began readying themselves for departure by the hundreds, King Charles I became concerned. In London, on February 28, 1634, ten ships were detained before they sailed, and their passengers were required to make an oath of allegiance to the king. Their captains were reminded that, among other obligations, they were to see that the prayers of the Church of England were read daily on the voyage.

One of the ten ships detained was the four-hundred-ton *Mary and John*, with Robert Sayres as captain. The *Mary and John* was a veteran of the New England crossing and had assisted already in the settlement of Dorchester, Massachusetts, and Windsor, Connecticut. After being delayed by a month, the passengers had finally all been sworn, and they were released to sail for Boston. Although a complete passenger list for the *Mary and John* has never been found, among the names of those thirty-eight sworn to obey the king were many of the first settlers of Newbury, including John Spencer, James and Nicholas Noyes, John Godfrey, Henry Lunt, John Woodbridge and Thomas Parker. The record is silent on the matter of wives, children and servants, since only free men were required to take the oath, but in previous voyages, the ship had carried between 140 and 150 people.

The *Mary and John* arrived in Boston in May 1634, and about one hundred of its passengers moved up the coast to Ipswich. How these new settlers passed the summer, fall and winter of 1634 is a mystery, though they must have been a great burden to the tiny town, which had been established only months before by ten families. By March 1635, three of these newcomers were well enough established to seek seats as representatives to the General Court from the town of Ipswich. The Court rejected Nicholas Easton and Henry Short and decided that "Mr. John Spencer only stands legally elected in the opinion of the Court."

Meanwhile, in September 1634, a group of Scottish and Irish dissenters sent letters to the colony asking for permission to settle between Ipswich and the Merrimack River. Permission was granted by the General Court that "the Scottish and Irish Gentlemen which intends to come hither shall have liberty to sit down in any place up the Merrimack River not possessed by any." Perhaps this was a reminder to the newly enlarged town of Ipswich that it would lose control of surrounding land that was not settled quickly. Though the Scottish and Irish group met with great difficulty during the crossing and ultimately abandoned their journey, this was not known to the residents of Ipswich, who faced losing the unsettled land to their north. That there would soon be a settlement along the Parker River was assumed in a grant made by the town of Ipswich in 1634, in a document granting permission for John Perkins to build a fish trap on the "Quasycung…but in case a plantation should there settle then he is to submit himself unto such conditions as shall then be imposed."

In the spring of 1635, the Reverend Thomas Parker and others whose names appear on the list of those swearing allegiance to the king aboard the *Mary and John* applied to the General Court for permission to settle Newbury. "Some of the chief of Ipswich desire leave to remove to Quascacunquen, to begin a plantation there which was granted them, and it was named Newberry." On May 6, 1635, the order was passed:

Monument to the first settlers of Newbury, erected in 1905. Photograph by C.D. Howard. *Courtesy of Historic New England.*

"Wessacucon is allowed by the Court to be a plantation…and the name of the said plantation is changed and hereafter to be called Neweberry." From the very beginning, Newbury was Reverend Parker's town, named for the community in England where he had last preached, and it was his family and neighbors who would form the core of the new settlement on the banks of the Quascacunquen River.

CHAPTER 3

WORKING THE LAND, GATHERING THE CHURCH

It is ordered that there shall be a convenient quantity of land sett out by Mr. Dumer and Mr. Bartholemewe within the bounds of Newbury for the keeping of the sheepe and cattell that came over in the Dutch shipps this yeare and to belong to the owners of said cattell.
—Order from the colony to the town, July 8, 1635

There is no record of exactly who first arrived in Newbury, or when or in what numbers. Based on the earliest documents available, along with the traditions passed down through the families of the first settlers, we may assume they left Ipswich by boat in May 1635 and landed on the north shore of the Quascacunquen. Joshua Coffin, in his 1845 history of Newbury, estimates that there were about forty settlers in this first boatload and passes on the tradition that Nicholas Noyes was the first to leap ashore. This landing has been commemorated for generations on May 8, but there is no record of the exact date of its occurrence. The landing place is now marked on the north bank of the Parker River with a commemorative boulder.

Reverend Parker seems to have been the uniting element of this first band of settlers, most of whom hailed from Parker's home community of Wiltshire, England. Several were also relatives of his, including James Noyes and John Woodbridge, who worked alongside Reverend Parker in the spiritual shepherding of the Newbury flock. Parker was a dedicated Puritan who left Oxford as a young man to live in exile with his father in Holland. He returned to England to lead "several devout Christians out of Wiltshire into New England."[4] Aged forty in 1635, Parker left such an impression on his flock that, twenty years after his death in 1677, the selectmen declared that

> the river called by the Indians Quasacuncon, and has since been called by diverse names, as Newbury river, Oldtown river, be from this time called by the name of the river Parker…[after] the first planter and pastor of the church of Newbury and learned schoolmaster.[5]

Parker would live to see quarrels and schisms rend his beloved congregation and even to be barred from leadership during one contentious year near the end of his long life; but in 1635, he was the unchallenged shepherd of a small, devoted flock.

Newbury townsfolk reenacted the landing of the first settlers as part of the 300th-anniversary celebration in 1935. *Courtesy of the Historical Society of Old Newbury.*

Stone marking the landing place of the first settlers. Parker River is in clear view. Photograph by George E. Noyes. *Courtesy of Historic New England.*

The "Father Stone," a carved stone figure, circa 1723. Though this is thought to be a likeness of Richard Dummer, it was carved over thirty years after his death. *Private collection.*

In addition to the *Mary and John* contingent, the Newbury settlers were joined by a young gentleman named Henry Sewell, who arrived with servants in tow. He had come over on the ship *Elizabeth and Dorcas*, but had also wintered in Ipswich. They were soon joined by Richard Dummer, a wealthy landowner from Bishopstoke, England, who had spent two years in Roxbury, where he had built a mill and a bridge and invested in the Castle Island Fort.

Richard Dummer's wife, Mary, provides the first glimpse of the religious conflict, sparked by dissidents like Anne Hutchinson, that would soon engulf all of New England. In Boston, in February 1636, Mary gave birth to a son, Shubael, and then fell gravely ill. Though Richard was in Newbury tending to considerable investments, he also appears to have been trying to stay out of Roxbury, where his wife's religious views were causing trouble; however, she convinced him to return to Boston, where she died. Missionary John Eliot's record of Roxbury church members describes Mary Dummer thus:

> *She was a Godly woman but by the seduction of some of her acquaintances she was led away into the new opinions in Mrs. Hutchinson's time and her husband removing to Newbury she there openly declared herself and did also (together with others' endeavors) seduce her husband and persuaded him to return to Boston; where she being young with child and ill...died in a most uncomfortable manner. But we believe God took her away in mercy from worse evil which she was falling into and we doubt not but she is gone to heaven.*[6]

Mary Dummer may have found Newbury a safe place to "openly declare herself" an adherent of Anne Hutchinson's unorthodox religious views, but that was before Parker and his Wiltshire flock had firm command of the banks of the river that would later bear his name. Hutchinson's heretical beliefs would not be tolerated in Newbury for long, and refusing to repudiate the convictions of his young wife would soon cost Richard Dummer dearly.

LAND ALLOCATION

Landing as they did in May, the settlers had many temperate months before them to build shelters, clear land and plant crops. Fish and game were plentiful, and their attentions would therefore have turned first to shelter. None of the very first houses in Newbury survive, though pieces of them are likely inside the walls and ceilings of later houses. Building materials, laboriously wrought, were often recycled through several houses and barns. Houses were moved, taken down, reassembled, attached to other buildings and sometimes demoted to outbuildings. They were never simply left to rot, unless entangled in a lawsuit or victimized by generations of neglect. Though there were certainly builders among the first settlers, the erection of timber-frame houses takes a

PLAN OF LOTS LAID-OUT TO THE FIRST SETTLERS OF NEWBURY, OLDTOWN —1635.

FROM AN ORIGINAL DRAWING MADE BY DANIEL DOLE IN 1828.

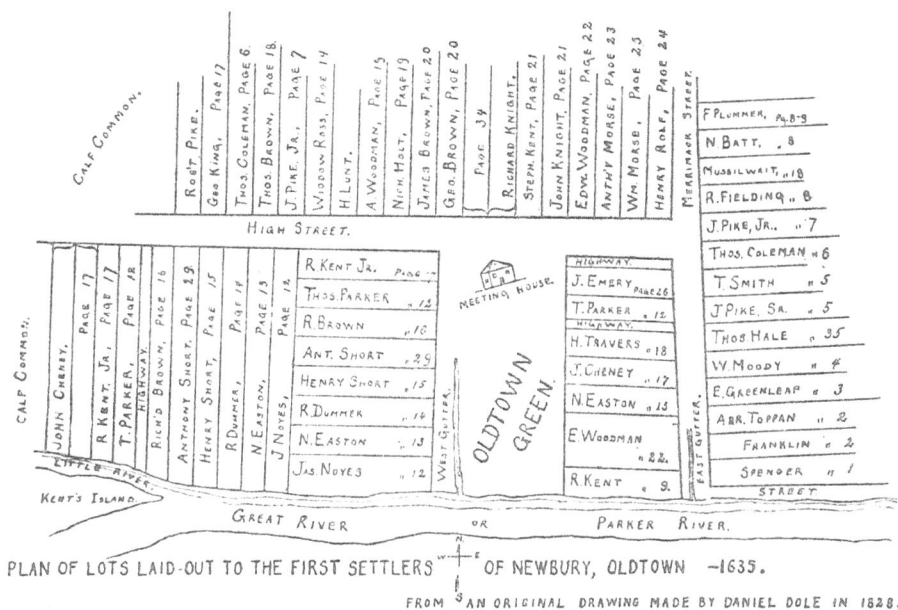

Plot plan of the first settlers. Note the calf commons and east and west gutters. Coffin's *A Sketch of the History of Newbury, Mass.*

matter of months in the best of times; with new settlers arriving daily, the immediate problem of shelter was likely met with a combination of tents, dugout sod huts and a sort of modified wigwam, copied from the light sapling and bark or hide dwellings of the local natives and covered with mud and sod.

While the problem of immediate shelter was being rectified, the company was busy surveying the land and laying out house lots, planting lots and meadow lots; the size of each granted lot was dependant on the amount of the owner's original investment in the company. House lots were set up along the river, surrounding the land now known as the Lower Green. Much larger grants of land were made to larger investors, often as planting lots and meadow lots: 400 acres to John Spencer; 1,080 to Richard Dummer; 630 to Henry Sewell; and other lots of varying sizes to other households, based on the rule that each settler would have a minimum 4-acre house lot and a right to pasture their animals on the common. Settlers who paid their own way were granted 50 acres, and others received 200 acres for every fifty pounds they had invested in the venture. Though women were not allowed to own land in their own right, widows and those conducting business in their husband's name were also granted lots.

No sooner had the first bounds been laid than ships began to arrive in Boston with passengers and cargo headed for Newbury. On June 3, 1635, three ships—two Dutch and one English—unloaded horses, cows and sheep, along with a number of settlers bound for Newbury. Richard Dummer was a principal investor in a joint sheep- and cattle-raising venture, and on July 8, 1635, the General Court ordered that land be set out by Dummer and his associates "for the keeping of the sheep and cattle that came over in the Dutch ships this year."

On the English ship *James*, one of the three that landed in June, Thomas Colman of Marlborough is listed as a "husbandman." Colman was hired by the venture to manage the herd of "certain horses, bulls, and sheep in a general stock for the space of three years." Within five months, however, many of the cattle were dead, victims of Colman's "exceeding negligence in discharging the trust committed to him, absenting himself from said cattle, and also neglecting to provide housing for them."

It is difficult to imagine simple starvation killing off large quantities of animals in a place like Newbury between June and November, when marsh grasses are at their peak, and even forested areas would have provided sufficient grazing for sheep and cows with room to roam. It is more likely that in absenting himself, Colman left the animals vulnerable to the natural predators in the area. Wolves roamed through Newbury for another 140 years, and bear, mountain lions and bobcats would have also taken their toll on the sheep and cattle. It is also possible that illness and the stress of the journey, intensified by months of relentless mosquito and greenhead infestation, caused the premature deaths of these animals.

Whatever the cause, the loss was a great blow to the fledgling plantation, and on November 3, 1635, Colman was relieved of his duties by the General Court, and the surviving animals were divided up and sent to live under the presumably more responsible care of their owners. The pasturing of cattle and sheep, and the division between common and private land, would continue to be issues until the final transfer of all common land was made in 1826.

With the first land divisions made and the cattle turned out to graze, residents spent that first summer furiously building houses and clearing land, and attention also quickly focused on securing business interests in the new town. Richard Dummer was not only one of the original cattle investors, but also, two months after settlement, he and John Spencer were given permission by the General Court to build a mill and fish trap at the falls of Newbury. This seems to have at first been a sawmill, since it came with timber rights. Three years later, Dummer was asked to outfit the mill to grind corn, with the promise that the town would send all of its corn to him exclusively and that there would be no other mill erected in Newbury.

Along with the mill, the fledgling community lost no time in securing a tavern, which not only served refreshment for the townsfolk, but also provided a place for travelers to stay. By September 1635, Francis Plumer was licensed to be the tavern keeper.

PLANTING THE CHURCH

In addition to its obvious economic interests, Newbury was essentially a Puritan community, and its inhabitants believed that they had been chosen to leave the corrupt and immoral Church of England and found an ideal godly community, their City on a Hill. This vision of community centered on the power and authority of devout, landowning men, in agreement with the established minister, assisted by their wives and able to control their servants and children. It also depended on a physical closeness, in order to ensure that the community worshipped together and kept an eye on each other. The church in Newbury was first gathered "on the Sabbath, in the open air, under a tree," according to testimony later in the century, when church relations were no longer so idyllic. On that Sunday, Reverend Parker was formally elected minister, and his cousin, Reverend James Noyes, was to assist him as teacher.

Headstone of Joshua Woodman, the first male child born in Newbury (in 1636) and the son of Edward Woodman. Next to him is Joshua Woodman Jr., his son. *Private collection.*

With the spiritual church gathered and house building under way, the community turned its attention to the erection of a physical church. This first meetinghouse was likely located just northwest of the Lower Green, with the burying ground adjacent to it first mentioned in a deed of 1647. Though the original building lasted for only just over a decade, it was the symbol of an ordered and godly town. The meetinghouse was the focal point for the growing community, and as that first uncertain summer came to a close, the General Court ordered that "no dwelling house shall be built above half a mile from the meetinghouse."

Thus, by the close of its first year, Newbury had divided the land, built a sawmill, opened a tavern and erected a meetinghouse. It also welcomed the first settler baby born in Newbury, a healthy girl named Mary Brown, who would live to be eighty-one years old. But the boundaries of Newbury were huge, forty thousand acres in all, and with new settlers arriving all the time, it would prove a great challenge to keep everyone together both in the spirit and in the flesh.

CHAPTER 4

AUTONOMY

Power Over Its Own Affairs

This year the general court enacted, that every particular township should have power over its own affairs, and to settle mulcts upon any offender upon any public order not exceeding twenty shillings, and liberty to chuse prudential men not exceeding seven to order the affaires of the town.
—Massachusetts General Court, 1636[7]

During the year of settlement, decisions involving the town were made by all of the freemen in common, though certainly, in a time when social status mattered a great deal, more weight would have been given to the opinions of those who had the greatest financial stake in the community. Since all the men who arrived with the initial company were given land unless they arrived in a state of servitude, they were all both *freemen* (members of the church who had been approved by the town and taken the freeman's oath) and *freeholders* (men who had not only been granted land, but also had a share in the common lands used for pasture, hay, fishing and so forth). Later, when all the land to be granted was gone, there was a brisk trade in the sale of freeholds, and the squabbling over who had the right to use common land became increasingly nasty. To make matters more complicated, in the initial scramble for land, some grants went unrecorded. The freehold of William Thomas, for example, was not recorded until 1643, when the land had been bought and sold; "although it was not set down in the list of the freeholders, they all acknowledged that it was forgot."[8]

In 1636, the General Court, overwhelmed with the oversight of thousands of quarrelsome new settlers, gave towns "liberty to choose prudential men, not exceeding seven, to order the affairs of the town." In towns like Newbury, these seven men became the first selectmen, and they had the power to oversee land grants, make town laws, accept or reject new settlers and issue fines. They officiated at town meetings, at which all freemen were required to vote on issues concerning the entire town. From the beginning, these meetings were contentious, and rules were strict. A moderator had the responsibility of keeping peace during the meeting and could be fined if he failed to do so successfully. Men stood up or removed their hats when they wished to speak, had to wait their turn and could not leave the meeting without permission. In addition to the affairs of the town, there were personal and business disputes to settle, and though petitioners could ask for a hearing at the quarterly Essex County courts, held in Salem and Ipswich, most local disputes were first brought to the home of a local magistrate, later called the justice of the peace.

In May 1636, Richard Dummer and John Spencer were chosen as magistrates in the town of Newbury. John Spencer was also appointed head of Newbury's military regiment, and tax was levied on the town by the General Court in the amount of eleven pounds, five shillings. This was about half the rate levied on the established town of Salem, for already Newbury was the seat of wealthy and prosperous men. With land transactions and town business booming, it was necessary to hire a "town register," or clerk. The twenty-two-year-old nephew of Reverend Parker, John Woodbridge, was given five pounds per year and was released from all taxes in exchange for keeping the books. John Woodbridge would play a major role in the bitter divisions that marked the end of his uncle's life, but for now, he worked hard and married well. In 1639, he won the hand of Mercy Dudley, the governor's daughter.

Freeholders—landowning men who were members of the church—were responsible for ordering the lives of their families and neighbors, and were selected, often without their consent, to attend to the endless variety of issues and tasks that the town required. In 1638, the town of Newbury appointed three men to "end small causes" in the town, as a way of sparing both the magistrates and the court system. The duties of such men in Newbury are unclear, but in Hampton (in today's New Hampshire), such men were empowered to

> *administer oaths in all civil cases; to issue warrants to search for stolen goods; to take notice of and punish defects in watching; to punish for drunkenness, excessive drinking, and such like crimes of an inferior nature, according to law; to bind over offenders to the county court; to solemnize marriages to persons duly published; and all this during the court's pleasure.*[9]

In 1645, the position was defined as having authority over any claim of less than twenty shillings.

Throughout these early years, groups of two or three men were appointed to lay highways, inspect fences and catch and imprison cattle and hogs that were a nuisance. They collected taxes, served as constables, surveyed lots, built bridges and organized the guard at the meetinghouse. When presented with a pressing need at town meeting, freeholders voted on a committee to oversee the project and its completion, often reducing their taxes or paying a small stipend if their duties entailed a serious time commitment. Participation on these committees was not optional, and members were often fined if they failed to complete their task. There was no separation of church and town and no distance between the personal and professional lives of its residents. The townspeople of Newbury kept a close eye on each other and were intimately involved in one another's lives.

The atmosphere in Newbury in the first few years of settlement was one of uncertainty and threat, from without and from within. Not only were new settlers arriving and seeking inclusion in town government, but there was also the constant threat of Indian attack, border pressure from the North and internal disobedience and strife. These threats were not exaggerated, and though a sustained Indian attack never materialized, in its first ten years of settlement, Newbury would see two murders, a kidnapping, two earthquakes and a plague of caterpillars.

Every aspect of Puritan life was governed by a search for signs of God's approval or reproach, and the devil was also at hand and able to make his presence known. In 1640, when John Godfrey, shepherd at John Spencer's farm, told William Osgood that he had agreed to work for a man whose name he could not remember, William assumed that John had made a deal with the devil. To the residents of Newbury, the meetinghouse was church, town hall, schoolhouse and social club. Where they sat in the meetinghouse, what they wore there and whether or not they came to every meeting were matters of great importance to all of the townspeople. It was also a setting for conflict. Brawls over pew assignments led to whippings for several young men later in the century, and shouting matches between feuding families—and later even between townsmen and the minister—were not uncommon. In 1638, John Pike was fined for "departing from the meeting without leave and contemptuously." The town records list fines for freemen who refused to come to meeting.

Natural disasters such as earthquakes and hurricanes caused serious soul-searching in the community, as well as providing great practical difficulties as trees blew over, chimneys and foundations cracked and floods washed away crops. The appearance of a comet or eclipse was cause for concern as well, as people tried to decide if it was a sign of blessing or trouble to come. On June 1, 1638, when an earthquake disrupted town meeting, John Woodbridge noted in the records that "all might take notice of Almighty God and fear his name."

RELIGIOUS CONFLICT

The first major conflict in the community was over religious orthodoxy. In August 1637, a group of ministers and magistrates met in Cambridge, concerned with weeding out religious beliefs contrary to those held by the Puritan establishment. Over eighty forbidden sects were listed by the group, including Baptists and followers of Anne Hutchinson, the charismatic female preacher whose teachings had so appealed to Richard Dummer's young wife. Followers of Anne Hutchinson held the dangerous belief that they were saved by grace and thus were exempt from moral and social law. The General Court moved quickly to stop the spread of these heresies, and ordered their adherents to be disarmed, "deprived of swords, guns, pistols, shot, and match."[10] Richard Dummer and John Spencer, whose names so often appeared together in those first two years, were disarmed, along with Nicholas Easton. Disarming was a serious punishment and was often a preliminary step toward further sanction. It was also insulting to men of their stature and robbed them of any military rank, not to mention the perils of going about unprotected in a countryside full of wolves, mountain lions and armed neighbors.

John Spencer and Nicholas Easton did not wait for further punishment. Spencer fled to England and never returned to the town in which he had invested so much. Easton fled to Rhode Island, that haven for heretics, where he later became governor. Richard Dummer left for England, but came back within a year, bringing with him eight family members, including his brother Stephen. Perhaps he had some private assurance that he was in no immediate danger; perhaps he felt that his investments were worth the risk; or perhaps he was tired of moving, having already left Roxbury for similar reasons. Whatever his reasons, Dummer lived under threat for an additional two years, until, in 1640, he had a chance to place Governor John Winthrop in his debt, thereby ensuring his standing in the community. Governor Winthrop's bailiff, who had been left in charge of his farm, accumulated £2,500—a fortune—in debt in Winthrop's name, and Winthrop was forced to sell much of his land to help pay it off. A call went out to wealthy landowners throughout the colony to make a voluntary donation for his relief. Richard Dummer contributed £100 of the £500 raised, more than the total taxes for the year for the town.

Although they never saw each other again, Richard Dummer continued to safeguard the interests of John Spencer in Newbury. Eleven years later, after his friend's death in England, Richard Dummer brought Spencer's will to the court at Ipswich and oversaw the transfer of his estate to his young nephew, also named John Spencer. Though Spencer was officially condemned, the town he left behind seems to have wished that he, like Dummer, would return. A land document from just after Spencer's departure bemoans his "intention and resolution to live away from us and so to deprive us of his usual help and council in managing and ordering our greatest and weightiest affairs." The fact that Spencer's land grant was kept intact, and that Dummer was allowed to return, indicates that they were both considered vital to the success of the fledgling community.

CRIME

In addition to crimes of the spirit, crimes of the flesh also needed policing in the growing colony. His own finances aside, Governor Winthrop wrote in 1640 that "as people increased, so sin abounded," and Newbury residents were no exception. As they toiled to build their City on a Hill, they came into conflict with each other over land, lovers, social status and business, and court records are full of Newbury residents accused of assault, slanderous language, destruction of property and sexual misdeeds.

Within a year of settlement, a young servant named Mary Sholy was sent from Newbury to join her master in Portsmouth. She did not want to go alone, and she asked a young man named William Schooler to escort her. Schooler returned after two days, claiming that he had dropped Mary off about three miles from her master's house after she "would go no further." Six months later, her body was found by an Indian ten miles shy of where Schooler claimed to have left her. Schooler was hanged in Boston in September 1637.

The first fornication trial in Essex County involved a Newbury man, Robert Coaker, who was presented in 1641, along with Miriam Moulton, of Hampton. Hampton had been settled by people from Newbury beginning in 1636, and it was likely that that was how the two knew each other. Coaker and Moulton had been engaged, and when Coaker broke off the engagement and married someone else, he was accused of fornication (sex between unmarried people), likely by Moulton, her family or the man she subsequently married. Because the two had been engaged at the time of the illicit acts, the court released Moulton without punishment, but sentenced Coaker "to be severely whipped," and to pay Moulton's husband five pounds, presumably as compensation for her virginity.

In 1644, William Franklin was arrested for beating, starving and eventually killing his young apprentice. Nathaniel Sewall appears to have been one of a number of children sent over from England without their families to work in Newbury in 1643. According to the court record, Franklin "used him with continual rigor and unmerciful correction," eventually tying Sewall to a horse and bringing him to Boston, where he died of the injuries inflicted by his master. Franklin's murder conviction was by no means assured, however, as he was a freeholder, and the corporal punishment of children—particularly servant children—was not only accepted, but also encouraged. At the second court session, however, the magistrates found him guilty, and he was hanged in Boston.

Thus, throughout this tumultuous first decade, even as they established themselves and attained a measure of local self-government, the people of Newbury were continually reminded of their sinful, and sometimes criminal, natures.

CHAPTER 5

THE PASSACONNAWAY AFFAIR, 1642

The military officers in every towne shall provide that watches bee dewly kept in places most fit for common safetie.
—*Massachusetts General Court, March 9, 1637*[11]

In addition to threats from within, the people of Newbury were keenly aware of the possibility of Indian attack. Every male settler was required to secure for himself a musket, powder and shot. In 1636, the General Court ordered that towns keep watch in "places most fit for common safety." The freemen of Newbury voted on this measure and determined that the best place to keep watch over the extensive lands of the town was from the top of Old Town Hill. Sentinels were stationed along this "walk of sixteen foot broad" to watch over the surrounding countryside.

The clearing of land, an arduous task today, even with the help of machinery, was backbreaking labor in the seventeenth century for men and oxen, but it must have taken on a special urgency when the security of the settlers' homes depended on it. At a town meeting in 1638, the possibility of building a fort near the first landing place was raised and a lot was reserved for that purpose, though it was never built. In June, however, the town decided that it needed to guard the meetinghouse, since it made an easy target when the entire community was gathered there. To that end, the town was divided up four ways, with a group from each quarter providing the armed guard for "one Sabbath day in a month and the lecture day following."

True to form, a committee was set up to ensure that each group took its proper shift, and shirkers were subject to being fined. That same year, the General Court sent Newbury a barrel of gunpowder and ordered that it should be "sold out to those that find muskets." Though they would never encounter Indians at their meetinghouse door, nine Newbury men were sent to Connecticut to fight in the Pequot War in 1637 and witnessed the reverse: the massacre of over six hundred native men, women and children.

In September 1642, it seemed that the threat from the native population was growing, and Governor John Winthrop distributed extra gunpowder (one more barrel for Newbury) and ordered that all Indians within the colony be disarmed. Of particular concern was Passaconnaway, a Pennacook sachem who lived farther up the Merrimack

The 1638 order for the protection of the meetinghouse. John Woodbridge and Edward Woodman both signed this document. *Engraved for Coffin's* A Sketch of the History of Newbury, Mass.

Powder house off Low Street (1822). The provision and storage of gunpowder was a constant concern to the early settlers. *Private collection.*

River. Aside from leading a band of armed men, Passaconnaway was rumored to be a sorcerer. "He can make the water burn, the rocks move, the trees dance, metamorphasize himself into a flaming man."[12] He was also allegedly able to produce a live snake from an old skin and grow green leaves from the ashes of dead ones. Filled with trepidation, a band of forty men from Newbury and Ipswich set out to disarm him.

From the beginning, the mission was a disaster. Paths were washed out by unusually heavy autumn rain, and the party was finally unable to make its way to Passaconnaway's dwelling; instead, they seized his son, along with a woman and child, presumably his daughter-in-law and grandchild. They tied the three together and marched them back to Newbury, but the son managed to slip off his ropes and disappear into the woods. The men returned to Newbury with the woman and child and sent notice to the General Court asking for instructions. They were immediately ordered to send the captives back, and "send to Passaconnaway for satisfaction."

The men had greatly overstepped their bounds in kidnapping the woman and child, and the Court grew very concerned about incurring the wrath of Passaconnaway. A delicate diplomatic mission was arranged, and several gentlemen who had taken no part in the kidnapping, along with guides and interpreters, went to Passaconnaway to explain to him that he was only to be disarmed temporarily, that his son had been taken "not by any order from us" and that "we have given order to have his squaw and papoose sent home to him again."[13] By the end of the month, the order to disarm was rescinded, and reconciliation with Passaconnaway was somehow achieved. In 1644, Passaconnaway and his sons sought the protection of the government and swore their allegiance.

The Newbury men had marched quite a distance upriver to find Passaconnaway and his family, into what is now Lowell, but there is evidence of a small resident native population in Newbury, probably never counting more than a dozen people. When lots in the "new town" closer to the Merrimack were laid out in 1644, lot 61 was reserved for "John Indian." On April 16, 1650, "great Tom, Indian" sold his rights to all lands in the town, including a substantial amount of fenced-in land under cultivation, known as Indian Hill.

Settlers and the courts debated the validity of native land rights throughout the seventeenth century, until all Newbury lands were purchased from Masconomet's grandson in 1701, but the resident native population had dwindled to just one family in Byfield by the 1660s. It was not local natives that the people of Newbury feared, but raiding parties from the north and west. In fact, the few native families who remained in Newbury in the first years seem to have looked to the settlers for protection. Though nearby towns, particularly Haverhill, were subject to attack, and Newbury men saw action in King Philip's War in 1675, no attacks were made on Newbury settlers until 1695.

CHAPTER 6

TRAVEL

Roads and Ferries

Granted to Aquila Chase anno 1646 four acres of land at the new towne for a house-lott and six acres of upland for a planting lott, where it is to be had, and six acres of Marsh, where it is to be had also, on condition that he do goe to sea and do service in the towne with a boate for four years.
—*Town of Newbury, 1646*[14]

Bounded as Newbury was on three sides by the Atlantic Ocean and the Parker and Merrimack Rivers, mobility was an immediate problem for the settlers. Though they had arrived from Ipswich by boat, they were not seafaring people; it was not until twenty years after settlement that they built a dock of any size, and until then, there were only a handful of people who owned or were familiar with watercraft. So pressing became the need for water transportation that, in 1646, the town granted Aquilla Chase six acres of land, "on condition that he go to sea and do service in the town with a boat for four years."

Though initially all energy in Newbury was concentrated on clearing land and building houses, there were constant, pressing needs and obligations that required travel outside Newbury. Courts were held in Salem and Ipswich. Magistrates and town representatives traveled regularly to sessions in Boston and Cambridge. Building materials needed to be brought to homesites, animals moved from winter to summer pasture, family members visited and, most importantly, church attended.

This difficulty of travel was to have a profound impact on the history of Newbury. Some of the most adamant and vicious conflicts in the town's history took place over the location of the meetinghouse, with its attendant burden of lengthy travel for those in outlying areas. For several years after the settling of Newbury, the only roads were narrow tracks, winding through woods and marsh along old game trails. People and animals that needed to cross the Parker River forded at low tide or swam. There were no ferries or bridges and no way to cross the Merrimack River except to hire a boat to navigate through the channels between the river islands near its mouth.

The town first focused on building roads. Many of the first acts of the town provided for the laying out and maintenance of roads, beginning with the "highway" between Newbury and Ipswich. All settlers were expected to work on the roads for a few days each year, and there are several recorded instances of townspeople hiring others to do

Tablet honoring Aquilla Chase, mariner. *Courtesy of the Newburyport Public Library.*

Salt marsh hay was often harvested by boat. *Courtesy of the Historical Society of Old Newbury.*

their share of the roadwork for them. Settlers seem to have preferred the improvement of their own land to working on the roads, and the General Court was so exasperated with their lack of progress that, in 1639, it ordered:

> *whereas the highways in this jurisdiction have not been laid out with such convenience for travelers as were fit, nor was intended by this Court, but that in some places they are felt too straight, and in other places, travelers are forced to go far about, it is therefore ordered that all highways shall be laid out before next General Court, so as may be with most ease and safety of travelers.* [15]

Laying out roads was tricky because, as the size and shape of the settlement changed, roads needed to be laid across lands already granted by the town. In 1640, the town gave the committees charged with surveying and awarding lots of land the power also to take land as needed for roads. The town was conscious of the outcry this would cause, however, and those who would benefit from a new road were expected to compensate the people whose land had been taken. This was not an easy business, and the town often faced angry freemen who demanded that they be given new land grants to make up for lands taken for roads.

House Built in 1728 by Samuel Seddon. To be used for the Entertainment of Travelers Crossing Oldtown Ferry. Newburyport, Mass.

Seddon Tavern, built in 1728 to serve passengers on the Parker River ferry. *Courtesy of Historic New England.*

THE PARKER RIVER FERRY

The first ferry in Newbury connected the town to Ipswich over the Parker River around 1640 and was built and operated by John Russe. It crossed the Parker River near the landing site and appears in the record in 1642, when Russe asked for compensation for two years' worth of transporting magistrates and deputies, "with their horses," from Dover, Salisbury, Portsmouth and Hampton across the Parker, on their way to and from court. The General Court paid him in 1642, but passed a law the following year making it compulsory for ferrymen to transport all persons on court business, along with their attendants, horses and baggage, for free. This seems to have been enough for Russe, who moved to Andover shortly thereafter and never returned to Newbury. Samuel Plummer took over the Parker River ferry and kept it in operation for the remainder of the century.

THE MERRIMACK RIVER FERRY

In the spring of 1636, the General Court, eager to assert its claim to the three miles of land north of the Merrimack River, ordered Richard Dummer and John Spencer to "press men to build a house forthwith" at Winnacunnet, now Hampton, New Hampshire. Dummer and Spencer quickly put up a boundary house, called the Bound House, and several Newbury families moved there. Salisbury, Hampton and Portsmouth could only be reached across the Merrimack River, and so, even with the larger share of Newbury citizens clustered around the Parker River, the search was on for someone to build a passable ferry over the Merrimack. In 1640, a committee of men was sent out to "settle the ferry where they think meet."

By 1641, George Carr, who lived in a house on an island in the river, was appointed to keep the ferry from Salisbury to Newbury. Carr's ferry proved to be unreliable, and Carr himself was brought before the court regularly for insulting passengers, refusing service and charging for cattle made to swim next to his boat. In 1641, he was presented for "suffering people to stand waiting at the waterside three hours to the prejudice of their health." Still, the redoubtable Carr family kept control of the ferry until 1696, and the island from which he plied his trade is named after him.

CHAPTER 7

GROWTH AND CHANGE

A New Town Center, 1642–1646

Generall and perticular orders made by the men Deputed for the Managing of those things that
concerne the ordering of the New Towne from Decem'b 7th 1642.
—Newbury Proprietors Records[16]

In the 1640s, population growth confronted the town with the need for a radical shift in its political geography. Newbury had naturally grown up around the first landing place, and the meetinghouse and burying ground were set up nearby. Thus, the town "center," rather than being in the middle of the settlement, was wedged into the southeast corner of it, bounded by the Parker River to the south and the Atlantic Ocean to the east. With the establishment of Rowley south of the Parker in 1639, Newbury had no choice but to spread inland to the north and west. By 1642, the mandatory twice-weekly meetings at the meetinghouse were increasingly difficult to attend for many newer residents, some of whom lived four or five miles away—no small distance on foot or on horseback.

Therefore, in 1642 the decision was taken to relocate the town center, meetinghouse and all. The first major step was to account for all men who had the right to common land, a major source of wealth since it allowed for the pasturage of valuable animals. Certain pasture rights, called "stints," for individual animals were assigned according to the amount of their owners' investment in the town, with separate common pastures set up for milk cows, the "dry" herd (young cows and those not in a milk cycle) and an ox herd for male animals. Each group was assigned a herdsman or shepherd, and in 1642, there were 563 "stints" for cattle in each of the three pastures, or almost seventeen hundred cattle total. Hogs were let loose to fend for themselves until fattened and slaughtered. This was not without problems, however, and the town was obliged to order all hogs to be ringed (to deter rooting) and yoked (to prevent them from breaking through fences). That hogs managed to survive running wild with rings in their noses and yokes around their necks is a testament to the fortitude of colonial swine.

In order to figure out how many places in the pasture each freeholder could have, a list was drawn up of all freeholders, fixing their rights "to no other persons whatsoever, except he get them by purchase or some other legal way." Any land not included in one of the ninety-two freeholds was to be "ordered to lie perpetually common."[17]

Swett's
March's } Tavern
Blue Anchor

Steven Swett
now Ilsly House

Muzzey's Lane

Abraham Toppan

Henry
Sewall
Tristram Coffin
Granted to Henry Travers 1645.
Sold to John Brown about 1659.
Sold to Henry Sewall 1660.

Meeting House

Road from first

Rev. Jas. Noyes.
Noyes' Lane, or South Street.

N

settlement at Parker River

Woodbridge's Farm

Emery's Lane.
Way to Mill.

Rolfe's Lane,

Robert
Morse.

Anthony
Morse

John Spencer Farm.

House

Richard Brown

Spencer Farm.

Spencer Farm

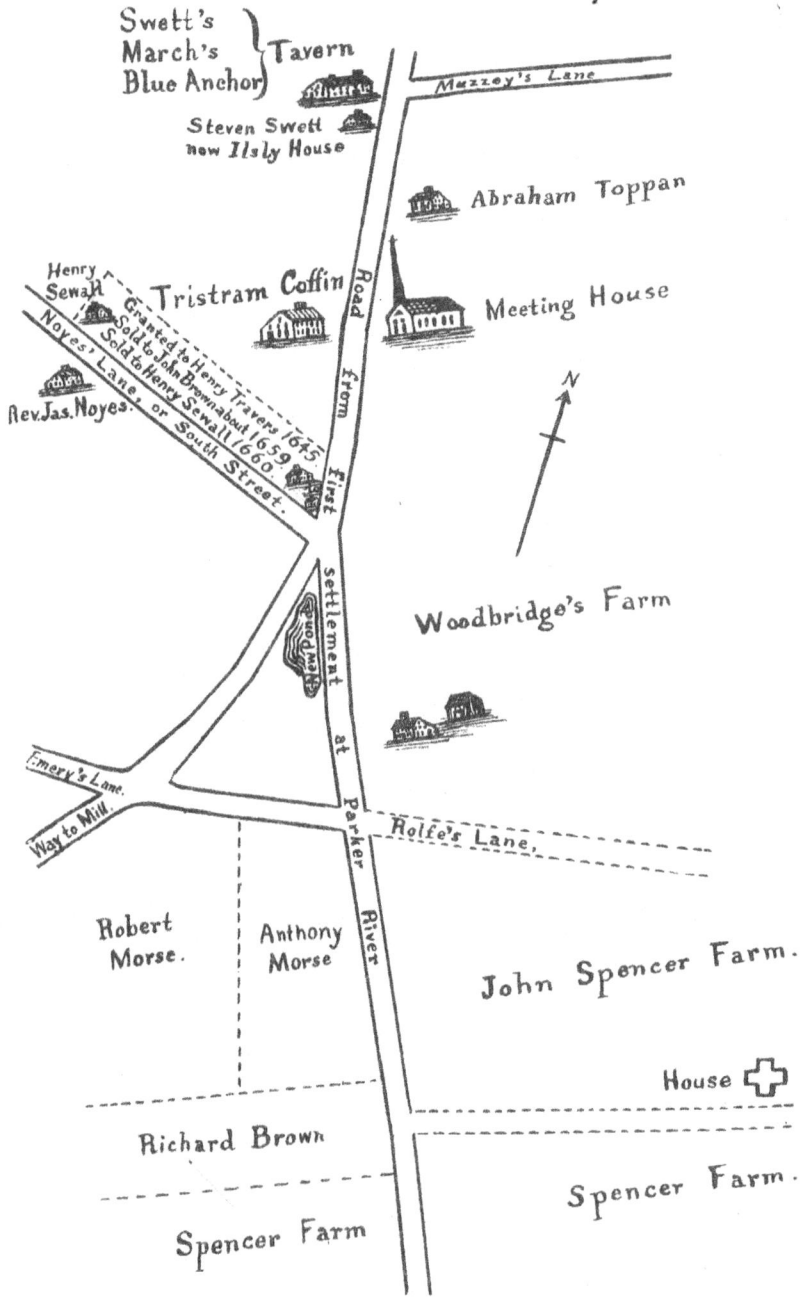

"TRAYNEING GREEN" AND NEW POND.

Plan of the upper green, where the meetinghouse, and therefore the town center, was moved in 1646. *From Currier's* "Ould Newbury."

View of the Lower Green from Old Town Hill. The landing place is near the center of this image along the water. *Courtesy of the Historical Society of Old Newbury.*

Freeholders were forbidden to let other people's cattle in with the Newbury herd, and they were not to exceed their own quota of cattle. Over six thousand acres within the bounds of Newbury were to remain common land, and as settlement ballooned later in the century, and the first Newbury families attempted to provide homesteads for their eight, twelve or fifteen children, the town was increasingly pressured to divide up the common land.

With the list of freeholders drawn up, the town, "well weighing the straits they were in for want of plow ground, remoteness of the common, scarcity of fencing stuff and the like," assigned the reverends Parker and Noyes, along with John Woodbridge and five other prominent men, to hunt for the best place for a new town center "for removing, settling, and disposing of the inhabitants." Another list was drawn up, this time to estimate the value of each man's house, "improved land" and goods, so that an equitable exchange could be made for land in the new town center. They decided that each freeholder would have a house lot of four acres and farmland in proportion to what they were relinquishing in the old town, with the smallest total grant being eight acres. They had the opportunity to start over, to lay out roads based on a known number of lots, to build fences before the hogs were let loose and to take advantage of the new ferry across the Merrimack to their sister communities to the north. They set the date of the move for 1646, giving the settlers four years to end their affairs in the old town.

Postcard view of the Toppan House, circa 1697. When the town center was moved north in 1646, the new meetinghouse was to be built "near Toppan's barn." *Courtesy of the Newburyport Public Library.*

Despite this apparently rational and well-ordered municipal planning process, the removal of an entire town, even one with only several hundred inhabitants, was a mammoth undertaking, and, almost immediately, conflicts arose over who was going to lay out the land, what was going to happen to the lots in the old town and where the meetinghouse was going to be located. From the beginning, there was a vocal minority—primarily those who lived near the old meetinghouse—that protested the move vigorously, taking the matter to the highest courts. In 1644, the General Court ordered that the town center should not be moved until a commission was set up to answer the petition sent by the Newbury men opposed to the action.

The selectmen moved ahead with the plan, however, attempting to placate the opposition by proposing that the meetinghouse be built closer to the old town than was initially proposed, "for settling the distractions that yet remain…that all men may cheerfully go on to improve their lands at the new town." This did not satisfy the plan's opponents, however, and in 1646, they sent a long, angry letter to the Court, demanding that the town's initial vote allowing the moving of the meetinghouse be rescinded, as it was "illegal and unjust." They spoke eloquently of the "sad sighs upon us when we consider how many thousand miles we are come" to settle in Newbury, and suggested that two meetinghouses be set up, one run by Reverend Parker and one by Reverend Noyes.[18]

The Court did not find their argument compelling and chided them for not "submitting to their own covenant" by doing what was best for the majority of the town.

After their petition failed, several of the petitioners left town, and they were immediately fined for not attending meeting. In December 1646, hinting at the trouble to come, Reverend Parker declared himself "unwilling to act in any matters concerning the new town," but the town, still attempting reconciliation, declared that town residents farthest from the proposed meetinghouse could choose to continue to live on their land, as long as "they go not to divide the church." Town meetings had grown so contentious that an outside moderator was appointed.

Meanwhile, the new town was laid out, sixty-six lots in all, with great concern being paid to fences, specifically that they be made strong enough to keep out swine and cattle. After much handwringing, it was decided to situate the new meetinghouse on "a knoll of upland by Abraham Toppan's barn," north of the upper green, in what is now the First Parish Burying Ground. The peace of the church had been spared—but only for the moment, as this fight over the location of the meetinghouse would turn out to be only the first of many.

CHAPTER 8

RESETTLEMENT

Land Records from Memory, 1646–1650

Whereas, by multitude of grants, sales, and exchanges by occasion of the townes removall have been Exchanged by the towne, and sold and exchanged one with another, and by the neglect of some severall grants that have not been recorded, for the prevention of all such abuses and unnecessary trubles, which are apt to arise therefrom, It is ordered that all and every inhabitant of this towne, that either looke at their owne profit or peace of the towne, shall at their owne perill repaire to Richard Knight and procure him, with some one of the eight commissioners, in case their evidence be not cleare otherwise, to testify to the towne clarke each grant made to any of them.
—Town of Newbury, Nov. 12, 1650[19]

If, in the first decade of its life, Newbury had nearly unlimited land, peaceful native neighbors and an unquestioning allegiance to Reverend Parker, the ensuing half century would be marked by increasing tension over land, Indian conflicts that would snatch a Newbury family from their home and a church in such crisis that the entire colony was called to intervene. Yet by 1700, the community was still primarily rural, with only two houses right on the Merrimack River.

In 1646, the center of town was moved northwest from the lower green to the Merrimack River. The new farm lots extended from the upper green in Newbury to the Artichoke River, with house lots set up between Federal Street and Market Street, the present-day heart of downtown Newburyport. There were always settlers pushing the boundaries, however. As early as 1644, John Emery gave his sixteen-year-old son an eighty-acre parcel of land along the Artichoke River, in what is now West Newbury. Though six thousand acres of land were set aside as common pasture until 1679, and though the Artichoke River formed a natural barrier that was not bridged until after 1704, various residents successfully petitioned for land grants along the road to Bradford, now Main Street, West Newbury. Although the town center was defined by the meetinghouse, there was no Port of Newbury on the Merrimack River in 1646, and the town was required to lay out both house and farm lots to all of its freeholders. The house lots were enormous by today's standards—four acres each—so even grouped together as they were, the new town was still very much a rural settlement. The primary reason for the move north was accessibility to good farmland.

Armed with the freeholder's list of 1642, the selectmen divided and allotted land as best they could, though the transient nature of early communities and the lack of

Curzon's Mill at the mouth of the Artichoke River, where John Emery Jr. previously had a mill. *Courtesy of the Historical Society of Old Newbury.*

reliable record keeping rendered the process more chaotic than intended. House lots were assigned according to the pleasure of the eight men charged with laying them out, and there was considerable swapping and selling. Once the issue of the meetinghouse was finally settled, and despite the best efforts of the lot layers, there was a scramble for the best land. By April 1646, the recording system had entirely broken down.

At their April meeting, the lot layers decided that

> *the time being too short to finish and perfectly record all the grants which have been made by the eight men, that whatever* [town clerk Edward] *Rawson shall record that himself or* [lot layer] *Richard Knight doth perfectly remember was granted to any inhabitant…shall be hereby acknowledged to be authentic and legal.*

The next four years were a chaotic time, and though deeds and grants were recorded, by 1650 the town compelled all of the landholders in Newbury to appear before Edward Rawson, the town clerk, to record all of their land transactions so at least they could be taxed appropriately. They also had to bring Richard Knight, so perfect was his memory, and pay him six pence for his trouble.

This order reveals how far the town had wandered from the well-ordered ideal. The City on the Hill was a free-for-all.

> *Whereas, by a multitude of grants, sales, and exchanges by occasion of the town's removal have been exchanged by the town, and sold and exchanged one with another and by the neglect of some several grants that have not been recorded, for the prevention of all such abuses and unnecessary troubles, which are apt to arise there from, it is ordered that*

all and every inhabitant of this town that either look at their own profit or the peace of the town [shall testify to their grant or risk losing it].

The process continued until 1661, when the lot layers were finally released, because "there is no more land to be granted by the town."

By the end of 1647, the move to the new town was completed, and the land on which the first meetinghouse had likely stood was sold for three pounds, with the exception of the burying ground, to John Emery. It is probable that the meetinghouse was taken down, and any salvageable materials were used in the construction of the new meetinghouse on the upper green. It would have been too tempting for the disaffected old-town men to occupy the building, and materials were valuable. In any case, the deed to Emery of the land makes no mention of the meetinghouse. Newbury had moved on.

CHAPTER 9

CIVIC ORDER

Keeping the Peace

*Wheras divers Complaints have been made from time to time of disorder in the meeting house, and
some endeavours have bin made to redresse it, and as yet none have taken effect, neither is it thought
that the abuses in the youth can bee so easily reformed, unless every housholder knows his seat in the
meeting house, Therefore the selectmen have taken it into consideration, and have endeavored to their
utmost to give all satisfaction, and accordingly doth hereby order that every housholder both men &
weomen shall sit in those seats that are appointed for them, hence forward dureing their lives, and not
to presse into seats when they are full already.*
—*Town of Newbury, January 24, 1651*[20]

In 1647, as the town was still settling into its new quarters, permission to keep a tavern
was granted to Tristram Coffin, who had emigrated from England five years before
with his wife, mother, five children and two sisters. Though he was a Royalist, supporting
the king of England in the conflict with Oliver Cromwell's Puritans, this does not seem
to have impeded Coffin's notably successful progress through the New World. He settled
first in Salisbury and then in Haverhill, whose deed of purchase from the Indians he
signed, and then spent twelve years in Newbury before eventually purchasing and
moving to Nantucket.

As for his contributions to Newbury, perhaps more important than his tavern business
was his obtaining the town's permission to run the ferry from Newbury to Carr's Island
in the Merrimack River, where the passengers would then be taken on to Salisbury by
George Carr. Tristram Coffin's ferry may have been a spur to the troublesome Carr to
step up his erratic service, and sharing the ferry business was clearly not to his liking. He
convinced the Court to return the entire service to him by offering to build a floating
bridge from his side of the island to Salisbury, so he would only have to ferry from the
Newbury side. Carr completed this bridge in 1655, and the General Court ordered that
"the other ferryman is hereby required to cease his ferriage."[21]

Dionis Coffin, Tristram's wife, ran the tavern (and cared for seven children) while he
was running the ferry. She was brought into court in 1653, accused of overcharging for
beer, but produced witnesses who testified that she used more malt than other brewers
and therefore made better beer, and she was released. By 1657, his ferry rights revoked,
Tristram and Dionis Coffin moved back to Salisbury, and in 1659, they left with Thomas

Judith Coffin's headstone, First Parish Burying Ground. Her stone bears an inscription noting that she lived to see 177 of her descendants. *Author photograph.*

Macy of Amesbury, their son Peter Coffin and several others and purchased the island of Nantucket for thirty pounds and two beaver hats.

They left behind their son, Tristram Coffin Jr., who at twenty-one had inherited the trade, wife and three children of first settler Henry Somerby; the wife being the fertile and hospitable Judith Greenleaf Somerby, with whom he would have an additional ten children. They both would have a significant role to play in the affairs of the town for the remainder of the century—Tristram, as a public figure, engaged in town affairs at every level, and Judith as the matriarch of a prominent family that would produce, in her lifetime, 177 members. Where Tristram and Judith Coffin began married life remains a mystery. When they married, he was twenty-one and she was twenty-eight, and she had control of her previous husband's sizeable estate. The house Tristram built in 1678 was across the street from the meetinghouse, and he would serve as its deacon for over twenty years.

The meetinghouse that was built in 1647 was a solid, square building, and church members were soon fighting over seat selection, since the best seats were a sign of social standing in the community. In January 1651, the selectmen acknowledged "diverse complaints, having been made from time to time of disorder in the meetinghouse." The situation seems to have degenerated into a turf war fought out between younger members

South view of the Coffin House, built by Tristram Coffin Jr. in 1678. The original house now forms the rear ell, with the south door the main entrance to a simple two-room structure. *Private collection.*

of feuding families, and the selectmen believed that "the abuses in the youth cannot be so easily reformed unless every house-holder knows his seat in the meetinghouse." The selectmen drew up a list, assigning every family a seat, and removed young men to seats at the rear of the building. They felt the need to specifically order the parishioners not to "press into seats where they are full already,"[22] suggesting an interesting picture of the "disorder" they were trying to remedy.

The use of intemperate language was also becoming a problem. William Snelling was presented to the court in 1652 for cursing. His crime was the recitation of this verse:

I'll pledge my friends
And for my foes
A plague for their heels
And a pox for their toes

The plague and the pox were too fresh in the memory of the people of Newbury to take this lightly. Just three years before, there had been a major, colony-wide outbreak of smallpox, and the deadly disease would continue to mow periodically through Newbury. When an outbreak occurred in November 1759, thirty-six people, almost all

By the nineteenth century, Enoch Flanders, Newburyport's town crier, was an entirely decorative figure. In seventeenth-century Newbury, the town crier provided the town with news, announced lost goods, followed ne'er-do-wells around announcing their crimes and appears to have carried a drum rather than a bell. *Courtesy of the Historical Society of Old Newbury.*

of them healthy adults, died within the month. Ironically, it was Newbury's primarily rural character that placed its citizens at greatest risk: the occasional wave of debilitating illness would often begin with settlers arriving from more densely populated areas of England, or even from Boston, where regular exposure to the pox built up an immunity in most people who lived to adulthood. In a rural community like Newbury, however, many children grew up without ever encountering the disease and were therefore struck down as adults, causing serious hardship for the community. In a community that believed in the power of invocation, summoning the pox was beyond the pale.

Friends of William Snelling rushed to his defense, testifying that he meant no harm and was simply reciting a proverb used in England; but the court was not amused, and it fined him ten shillings and court costs.

Snelling was not the only Newbury resident who was told to watch his mouth. In the same session, Elizabeth Randall of Newbury was charged with calling Goodwife Silver a "base lying devil, base lying toad, base lying sow, and base lying jade." Elizabeth Randall was no stranger to the court, and the key to her outburst at Goodwife Silver may lie in her presentment for fornication the year before. In October 1650, Elizabeth and her husband, William, were presented at court for having a baby ten weeks early. When the midwife arrived, William denied that the baby was his, claiming not to have had sexual relations with Elizabeth before their marriage. When pressed, William admitted that the baby could be his, and "from six or seven weeks before marriage he would own the child to be his."[23] This would still require the baby to have been a month early, certainly enough to cause gossip in the community. There is no record of how either case was settled, but Elizabeth Randall appears again in court records more than a decade later, charged with disturbing services at the meetinghouse because she didn't get the seat she wanted. "Although she had been granted another seat, superior in dignity, she proceeded to press [into her old seat], and altogether unbecoming her sex, to climb, ride, or stride over, it being four or five feet high, and to force the door." When she didn't get her way, she sat down in the aisle.[24]

Another thorn in the side of the women of Newbury was the General Court's sumptuary laws, which sought to keep people from dressing above their social station. In 1651, the Court declared

> their utter detestation and dislike that men of mean conditions and callings should take upon themselves the garb of gentlemen by wearing gold or silver lace, or buttons, or points at their knees, to walk in great boots, or women of the same rank to wear silk or tiffany hoods or scarves.

This gave quarrelsome neighbors another way to keep tabs on each other, and when Richard Knight's wife was presented for wearing a silk hood, he blamed "ignorance or willfulness of some neighbor." By 1653, six Newbury women were subjected to the humiliation of proving in court that they had a right to wear fine clothing, either by proving the value of their husband's estate or by arguing that they were "brought up above the ordinary rank."[25]

Occasionally, quite prominent members of the community could become a public nuisance. Henry Sewell, a stalwart early settler of Newbury, had moved to Rowley when the meetinghouse moved, and from 1645 on, he seems to have suffered from an increasingly combative dementia. The quarterly courts were often called upon to deal with Sewell, beginning with an admonishment for disturbing the minister and followed by regular fines and punishments. He was made to read apology letters in the meetinghouse and post bonds for good behavior. In September 1650, he was fined for disturbing a public meeting and "doing violence upon the son of William Acey and drawing blood."[26]

Sewell's case offers a rare glimpse at how those who suffered from mental illness were treated by their fellow citizens and by the courts. In the fall of 1650, Henry Sewell walked into the meetinghouse and straight up to the front of the church. When the minister told him to stop, he ignored him, and when the minister reminded him that they were in the house of God, Sewell replied that he knew how to act in the house of God as well as anyone else. The minister asked that he be removed from the meetinghouse, and Sewell dared any member of the congregation to throw him out. Eventually he was removed from the meetinghouse, but he continued to attend and often made a spectacle of himself. At nearly every quarterly court, he was brought in, put up a bond for good behavior and forfeited the previous bond. In 1652, the court simply instituted a payment for each month, to be forgiven if he came to court with a certificate of good behavior from the selectmen. For the remainder of his life, Sewell was brought into court for beating up one neighbor or another, and each time he was released, the court being unwilling to further punish him.

When Henry Sewell finally died in 1657, his inventory listed a debt to "goody Bradstreet for twelve weeks [of] surgery, and taking pains in changing linen, he not being able to help himself in his bed," and to Richard Swan for "twelve weeks tending and wood, washing, and provisions."[27] Henry Sewell was a fairly wealthy man who had once been an upstanding member of the Newbury community. He was never whipped, never made to sit in the stocks and never imprisoned. There was simply nowhere for him to go but home again. His neighbors lived with his behavior and tended to him to the end of his life.

Preaching Out of Turn

Not only did the good people of Newbury fight with one another over where they were going to sit in the meetinghouse and what their neighbors were wearing, but they also found occasion to fight with the General Court. In 1653, the Court passed a resolution making it illegal for anyone to preach in any town in the colony without the permission of the Court or four elders in the community. In the absence of a minister in West Salisbury (now part of Amesbury), Thomas Macy and Joseph Peasley had taken to preaching there on Sundays and refused to discontinue this practice when ordered. (Thomas Macy would leave in 1659 with Tristram Coffin Sr. to settle Nantucket, but not until he had gotten into more trouble with the religious authorities for entertaining Quakers.)

Taking Macy and Peasley's side was twenty-three-year-old Lieutenant Robert Pike of Salisbury, son of one of the first settlers of Newbury, who railed publicly against the Court's order, denouncing it as, among other things, an unwarranted interference with the rights of freemen. He declared that "such persons as did act in making that law restraining unfit persons from constant preaching did break their oath to the country, for it is against the liberty of the country, both civil and ecclesiastical."[28] He charged that several churches had called their General Court representatives in for questioning, and "some places were about to show their mind to the General Court about it."

Punishment was swift and severe. Pike lost his status as a freeman, was prohibited from holding public office and was fined over thirteen pounds, a very high sum. If the Court's original law did not inspire the public outcry that Pike hoped for, his treatment by the Court certainly did. Petitions circulated through neighboring towns, and fifty-eight of Newbury's most prominent men, including Richard Dummer and Tristram Coffin Sr., signed it. They asked

> that whereas our loving friend...hath let fall some words for which the honored Court hath been pleased to censure him, we having had experience that he hath been a peaceful

man and a useful instrument…do therefore humbly desire this Court that the said sentence may be revoked.

The petition did not have its desired effect. In fact, the Court was incensed that towns would question its authority, and it formed a committee of investigation to root out Pike's supporters, saying that "this Court cannot but deeply resent that so many persons of several towns, conditions, and relations, should combine together to present such an unjust and unreasonable request."[29] Local commissioners were appointed to "require a reason of their unjust request." The men of Newbury had a variety of reasons for their support of Pike. Several argued that it was within their right to petition the Court, and all the Court had to do was reject the petition. Several said they were friends of the family and were unaware of the gravity of his offense.

When they showed up at John Emery's house, he demanded to see their commission and then told them that they had no right to ask who had first brought it to his attention. "His carriage, we conceive, was insulting," the commissioners wrote in their report. The Court levied the very large fine of ten pounds on those men whose answers to the commission were not adequate, including, not surprisingly, John Emery. He and his family would appear many more times in the court records for defying the authorities by entertaining strangers and sheltering Quakers.

Six months later, the Court revoked the offensive law, but did not mitigate the punishments. Robert Pike was forced to pay his fine and was not allowed to participate in community affairs until four years later, and then only because the minister vouched for him. The General Court was not to be trifled with, and it took its responsibility to keep order and enforce religious orthodoxy very seriously.

BRIDGE, MILL AND WHARF

Around 1654, Newbury also secured its first bridge over the Parker River, and the General Court declared that "Richard Thorlay [Thurlow], having built a bridge over Newbury River, at his own cost, hath liberty to take toll for cattle, sheep, and so forth…passengers free."[30] Eventually, however, this enterprise proved to be more than Thurlow could handle, and in 1670, the county court noted that, "the bridge and way in Newbury…being in many places bad and dangerous, the court orders Captain William Gerrish and Daniel Peirce Senior be empowered to see the way sufficiently improved."[31] There was no highway crew to do this work, and the court ordered that Gerrish and Peirce press the inhabitants of Newbury into service to mend the road. If anyone refused, they were to be brought before the court.

Many of these early enterprises were a confusing mix of private initiative and public funds. A bridge, highway or mill could be owned by a family, repaired by the town and have its rates set by the county. Promises of exclusive rights were often granted to

View of the lower green across the Parker River Bridge, also the site of the Parker River ferry. Photograph by S.C. Reed. *Courtesy of Historic New England.*

encourage businesses to set up in Newbury, and then, as the businesses were overwhelmed or fell into disrepair, other enterprising men were allowed to take over.

Population shifts also necessitated new arrangements, and after the town center moved, Richard Dummer's mill was too far to travel for many of Newbury's citizens. In 1645, John Emery and Samuel Scullard were granted the right to build a mill on the Little River, closer to the new center of town. They were given a very good deal for their efforts: twenty pounds in "merchantable goods," ten acres of upland and six of marsh, seven years of tax exemption and possession of the land in freehold "to them and their heirs forever."[32] However, some version of Dummer's mill continued to serve the citizens of Rowley and Byfield well into the twentieth century, as a corn mill, sawmill and ultimately a fulling mill, used to process the wool of the many thousands of sheep that roamed through the common pastures.

In 1656, the town encouraged another riverine enterprise, this one by the Merrimack, granting Captain Paul White half an acre of land "about Watts his cellar, for to make a dock, a wharf, and a warehouse." This did not come with a freehold, however. Captain White was a relative newcomer, having been in Newbury for only two years, and the town was still skeptical about the maritime trade that would become its lifeblood in later years. White did build his wharf, improved it by adding a distillery and continued his trade there until his death in 1679.

CHAPTER 10

PERSECUTING THE QUAKERS

Mr. Edmond Batter admonished on his presentment for saying that Eliz Kitchin had been
"apawawing" and calling her base quaking slut, with divers other opprobrious and taunting speeches.
—Essex County quarterly court records, 1660[33]

The first Quakers, two female missionaries, arrived in Boston in 1656 and were imprisoned and sent back to England. Strenuous efforts were made to ensure that they spoke to no one: boards were nailed up over their prison bars, and their books were burned. As more Quakers arrived, every attempt was made to ensure that they did not have the time or the opportunity to spread their "dangerous, heretical, and blasphemous opinions," and they were arrested, imprisoned and deported. If they returned, they could be whipped and have their ears cut off and their tongues bored through with hot irons. Stiff penalties were also levied on any member of the colony who provided them with food or shelter.

The Quakers were particularly dangerous to the established order in the colony because they did not recognize the authority of the established church, and they believed that all people—men and women alike—could communicate directly with God. Puritan society was rooted firmly in the idea of church discipline, and although relations within the church were often quarrelsome and contentious, the idea that one could simply drop out of the system was unimaginable.

Despite the authorities' best efforts to suppress them, however, Quakers managed to slip into the colony, and in 1658, they made it to Salem. Quakers William Brand and William Lutherway hosted a meeting in March on a Sunday, and many of the town's prominent citizens attended—ensuring that they would be caught, since their absence at meeting would be noted. When the constable arrived, the Quakers escaped, but were later caught and thrown in jail.

Brand and Lutherway were interrogated by the court and asked their business in the county, but it is the reaction of the townspeople who met with them that is perhaps most striking. "Many came into court with their hats on, and stood with them on until an officer pulled them off."[34] Many women attended without their husbands, some with their children. Some refused to come to court. They all were charged with "absence from meeting" and fined, but the court quickly turned to the issue of belief. All subjects were interrogated, and those who admitted to Quaker sympathies were fined or thrown in jail, or both. For the next several years, hundreds of entries in the court records make note of the absence of townspeople from public meetings, many of them specifically identified as Quakers. Some were fined, some were put in the stocks and the ringleaders were whipped and imprisoned in Boston.

The first recorded Quakers in Newbury appear in June 1659, when the court paid costs to transport two Quakers from Newbury to Salem, where they would be "sent to Boston Jail." In the summer of 1659, Thomas Macy, one of the men whose preaching in Salisbury had caused Lieutenant Pike such trouble six years earlier, was prosecuted by the General Court for entertaining Quakers. In a letter sent to the General Court, he excused himself from appearing in person, but related his case:

> *On a rainy morning, there came to my house Edward Wharton and three men more…I never saw any of the men except Wharton, neither did I require their names, or who they were, but by their carriage I thought they might be Quakers and told them so and therefore desired them to pass on and as soon as the violence of the rain ceased (for it rained very hard), they went away and I never saw them since. The time that they stayed in the house was about three quarters of an hour, but I can safely affirm it was not an hour.*[35]

Two of the men who were with Edward Wharton that rainy morning were William Robinson and Marmaduke Stephenson, both recently arrived from England.[36] Both were hanged in Boston on October 27, 1659. Even letting Quakers get out of the rain for forty-five minutes was a serious offense, and Macy was fined and ordered to report to the governor to be "admonished." He packed up his family and a few household possessions and left for Nantucket, which he had purchased with Tristram Coffin Sr. earlier that year. Thomas Macy had been trouble for years, and he is referred to in court documents as a "Baptist." By the end of the century, Nantucket had become a haven within the colony for religious nonconformists, and in later centuries, the majority of its inhabitants were Quakers.

Among many other instances of persecution of Quakers, in Salem in 1660, wealthy landowner Edmond Batter pulled Elizabeth Kitchin off her horse and called her "a base quaking slut."[37] Although he was found to have done so wrongfully, in 1661, Quaker laws in the colony were tightened further, ordering that Quakers, men and women alike, were to be seized, "stripped naked from the middle upwards and tied [behind a cart] and whipped through the town."[38] Quakers in England petitioned the king for leniency, but by 1662, English Quakers were causing enough trouble in the old country that the king gave permission for the colonies to continue "to make sharp laws against them."

In 1662, two Quaker women, Mary Tompkins and Alice Ambrose, along with two men, passed through Newbury on their way to Dover. They found a friendly reception in Newbury at the home of John Emery, who had earlier, similarly to Robert Pike, defied the right of the courts to restrict preaching to approved ministers. According to *New England Judged*, published in 1703, the four stopped "in their way through Newbury and went into the house of one John Emery (a friendly man), who with his wife seemed glad to receive them, at whose house they found freedom to stay all night."[39]

During the night, someone alerted Reverend Parker to the presence of Quakers in his town, and he came with a group of men to the Emerys' house first thing in the morning. They argued and debated for several hours, until one of the Quaker women's stomach growled loudly, "she having received no sustenance for the space of near forty-eight hours." Some of the men concluded that "she had the devil in her," and Parker took the Emerys out of the house and "began to deal with them for entertaining such dangerous people." John and Mary Emery relied on the longstanding tradition of hospitality, so necessary in frontier communities, where a place to stay for the night could mean the difference between life and death. They argued that they were required to entertain travelers, and Parker replied that these Quakers "had plague sores upon them." Mary Emery took offense to this and accused him of "false, wicked, and malicious words," and Parker, seeing that he was getting nowhere, left hurriedly, while one of the Quaker women called him a coward for leaving.

The women left later that day, and in December, two of the women were among three ordered to be tied to a cart and whipped from Dover, New Hampshire, through Newbury and on through Boston and out of the colony, a process that would almost certainly have killed them. They were whipped through Dover, Hampton and Salisbury, but when they got to Newbury, several men took pity on the cold, bleeding women and released them, claiming that they could not be whipped in more than three towns.

John Emery and his wife, though by all accounts upstanding members of their church, continued to openly entertain Quakers. In 1663, James Noyes (son of the deceased reverend) ran to Emery's house to tell him that two Quakers were on their way and to beg him not to let them in. Emery said that "if they came to his house they would be welcome and he would not forbid them." James Noyes testified that Quakers were "entertained very kindly to bed and to table and John Emery shook them by the hand and bid them welcome." There is no record of a verdict in these cases. He was most likely fined, since more severe punishments were reserved for those who had converted, and he was still a member of the church.

Though there was a long tradition of hospitality in Newbury, unattached, landless strangers were viewed with great suspicion, and the town was responsible for their care if they managed to stay for more than three months without being "warned out." In order to avoid accepting dubious characters into the town, householders were not allowed to let a nonresident live with them for more than twenty days without notifying the selectmen. These laws were often violated, particularly when whole families were allowed to rent property, putting the town at risk of supporting widows and orphans. John Emery got himself into trouble again in 1663 for hosting Henry Greenland, a different kind of stranger.

CHAPTER 11

SCANDALOUS BEHAVIOR

I said did not you nor goody Roffe se him put of his Clothes before he Cam in to bed: she answered
no for she was unreking the fier fore she said she had newly Raked it up and thought Mr. Grenland
had stood behind hir: and she said goody Roffe was a bed feeding her child with her bac towards the
fier…Betie said goody Rofe was so afrighted that she fell into a greevios fitt.
—*Essex County quarterly court records, 1663*[40]

D r. Henry Greenland came over from England to Newbury in late 1662, leaving his wife behind. He chose Newbury because a man of his acquaintance named Captain Walter Barefoot was living in town. Captain Barefoot was a fur trader and maverick with business relationships and pending court cases from Boston to Portsmouth. He carried a sword, dressed as a gentleman and liked a stiff drink and a good fight. Captain Barefoot was present when Robert Pike released the Quaker women when they were whipped into Newbury the year before, and he clearly had a close acquaintance with the Emery family. John Emery took the doctor in, hoping to induce Dr. Greenland "to settle and make use of his practice of physic and surgery among us."

Greenland had nowhere to live, and he was waiting for his wife to arrive before making any permanent decisions. The elderly John Emery became dependant on his care, and the fervor with which he later pleaded to have Greenland returned to him suggests that his ministrations were unusually successful, or addictive, or both. Greenland also saw other patients at the Emery house and developed quite a following. In 1663, John Emery was turned in for allowing Greenland to live with him for four months, and he was fined four pounds, plus costs and fees "for entertaining strangers." This was far above the usual fine for this violation, but Greenland was a particularly troublesome character. Emery fought the fine, presenting a petition signed by forty Newbury men, arguing that "the gentleman hath (by God's blessing) been instrumental of much good." Emery's fine, though upheld by the upper court, was reduced to court costs, and he was sent home.

Greenland had caused a great deal of trouble for the Emery family, not only by remaining illegally in their house, but also by aggressively pursuing a young married woman whom John Emery had sworn to protect. Shortly after his arrival in Newbury, Greenland set his sights on Mary, the young wife of John Rolfe, who had left to fish off Nantucket. Mary Rolfe went to the Emery house and asked Emery's stepdaughter, Betty

Webster, to stay with her while her husband was gone. John Emery promised to take care of them both "like my own daughters" in John Rolfe's absence.

Unfortunately for Emery, however, Mary Rolfe was "merrily disposed" and a bit of a flirt, and she was impressed with Greenland's quick wit and aggressive behavior. One night, while John Emery said the blessing over dinner, Greenland interrupted him with "Come, landlord—light supper, short grace," a quip Mary found quite amusing. When he grabbed her apron, she let him draw her to him "to save the apron."

Several nights later, Greenland came knocking on Mary's window late at night, saying he "would do no hurt, but desired to smoke a pipe of tobacco." Betty Webster let him in, and when she turned to tend the fire, he stripped naked and jumped in bed with Mary Rolfe. Mary screamed and fainted, and Betty accused him of giving Mary fits. Greenland replied, "It is nothing but a mad fit," but he got out of bed. When Mary protested that she was not mad, Greenland jumped in again. Hearing the commotion, a neighbor's servant, Henry Lessenby, crawled through a window into the house, but decided, along with Betty Webster, that it was a private matter and best not to make a fuss. Lessenby had been sued for slander by Dr. Greenland for testifying that he had heard Greenland contemplating the seduction of a Hampton woman, and he may have feared another slander trial if he spoke up again.

Mary Rolfe's mother caught Greenland at her daughter's house a few days later and was appalled. Still, the doctor's status as a gentleman and his good reputation made it difficult to press the issue, and rather than turn Greenland in herself, Mary's mother looked to John Emery for moral guidance. He refused to make a complaint against the doctor, but promised to keep an eye on him and to lock the liquor cabinet, blaming the doctor's behavior on drunkenness. Mary's mother argued that if he had been drunk, he would have stayed in bed rather than molesting her daughter. Emery replied that "he was half drunk and then was worse than dead drunk."

In fact, John Emery seems to have been willing to allow the seduction to continue; he even allegedly brought Greenland to Mary Rolfe's house on one occasion and left him there. John Emery himself had been convicted of adultery in 1646, just before the death of his first wife, and he seems to have been very liberal in all of his beliefs. Emery ran a very merry household, allowing men and women to be alone unsupervised and providing quantities of liquor to his guests. Mary Rolfe was not entirely blameless, in any event. On one occasion, she was heard to say that she was saving some wine until Dr. Greenland came home, "for she said he seemed to be a pretty man and she desired to be acquainted with him." In fact, she had been part of an earlier court case in which a friend of Greenland's, Richard Cordin, had attempted to seduce her in her mother's barn.

John Emery's wife, Mary Emery, who had stood by his side when it came to Quakers, was not so enthralled with Greenland, and she encouraged Mary Rolfe's mother to go to the authorities, which she did. Mary Emery also, on several occasions, tried to convince Mary Rolfe "not to carry herself so lovingly and fondly toward Mr. Greenland." But when it was clear that her husband's role in the relationship would be revealed in court, she tried to convince Betty Webster to withdraw her testimony. Some of Betty Webster's testimony was eventually disproved in court, and she was sentenced to "stand at the meetinghouse door in Newbury the next lecture day…with a paper on her head, written in capital letters FOR TAKING A FALSE OATH."

This did not help Greenland's case, however. Greenland was tried by a jury, and though one witness argued that "he had been a soldier and was a gentleman, and they must have their liberties," he was found guilty of attempted adultery. He was sentenced to prison and whipping, but was released with a bond of good behavior and a whopping thirty pound fine. His friend Captain Barefoot put up his bond for good behavior.[41]

The Naked Protester

Though a juicy sexual scandal could certainly command the town's attention, it was the Quakers who continued to obsess the quarterly courts in the early 1660s. Constables in Lynn, Marblehead and Newbury applied to the court for additional payments for apprehending Quakers and bringing them to court. A special judge was appointed whose sole task was to hear cases of townspeople who were absent from the meetinghouse and, if they were found to be Quakers, to issue fines and enforce them.

Newbury citizens do not appear in the court records accused of being Quakers in great numbers, but one of their own who had converted caused possibly the greatest scandal and disruption of any Quaker. Lydia Wardwell had been a member of the church of Newbury, but had married a Hampton man and converted to Quakerism. She seems to have been very upset at their fines for not attending church, and in April 1663, she walked into the Newbury meetinghouse and stripped naked in protest. Nakedness had been used by Quaker women as a protest before, but never in the meetinghouse itself, and she was arrested and sent back to Hampton. In May, she was brought before the Ipswich court, fined for the costs of the constable who brought her from Hampton and "severely whipped."

The pro-Quaker George Bishop, in his book *New England Judged*, claims that

> *without law they condemned her to be tied to the fencepost of the tavern where they sat, and which is usually the place for their court, where they may serve their ears with music and their bellies with wine and gluttony, whereunto she was tied, stripped from the waist upward, with her naked breasts to the splinters of the posts, and there sorely lashed with twenty or thirty cruel stripes.*[42]

Though the picture of half-drunk, gluttonous judges is doubtless overdrawn, courts were commonly held in taverns, and the whipping post would have been close by. Though Lydia's version of events does not appear in the record, Bishop lays out the hardships suffered by her husband, who lost his horse, his cattle, his corn and, eventually, his land because of his religious beliefs. Though her actions were certainly exaggerated, her complaints were not. Many Quakers lost everything, one fine at a time, and eventually Lydia and her husband fled, with many others, to Rhode Island.

The Newbury meetinghouse that Lydia Wardwell so scandalized was new in 1663. The building constructed in 1647 had become too small, and the new structure was laid out next to it in 1661. It was a very large building, with a three-tiered gallery, "three pair of stairs" and a bell. The old meetinghouse continued to be used while the new one was built, and then it was gutted and taken down. Its parts were either used in the new building or sold. Seats in the new meetinghouse were allocated by the selectmen, and, true to form, fighting immediately erupted over seating assignments. In 1663, four men were brought to the county court for "coming into the seats of other men contrary to the order of the selectmen." They were released upon promising to behave, but to be certain, in 1664, Giles Cromwell was hired "to keep the boys in order in the meetinghouse and to give notice to selectmen of such as are out of order."[43]

Even the social order of the parishioner's horses was of grave importance, with residents jockeying for the best hitching spot. Some petitioned the town for permission to build a barn near the meetinghouse, while the rest fought for a prime spot along the front fence. When the selectmen ordered that no horses could be tied to the outside of the fence, since they were getting in the way of orderly progress into the meetinghouse, they were shocked to find all of the horses tied up inside the fence on the following Sunday. This led to the adoption of the order that "no horses shall be tied within side or without side of the fence."[44]

DR. GREENLAND BANISHED

While tempers at the meetinghouse flared, down the street, Stephen Swett's tavern was the site of a bloody brawl, starring the notorious Captain Barefoot and Dr. Henry Greenland. In the summer of 1664, Barefoot and Greenland were drinking in the tavern when an Indian named Sesegenaway walked in. Barefoot had sued Sesegenaway for some furs he felt were owed to him, but the case was unresolved, and when Barefoot saw him at the tavern, he called on his friend Greenland to restrain him and send for the constable. Meanwhile, Barefoot went into a back room and filled out an "attachment," a document that gave the constable the right to take bodily possession of Sesegenaway.

Richard Dole, a prominent citizen whose servant had testified against Greenland at his earlier adultery trial, and Stephen Swett, the owner of the tavern, came into the room where Barefoot was filling out the warrant and questioned his right to seize Sesegenaway, asking him if he was "a clerk of the writs." Barefoot retorted that he "would prove [Dole] the verriest knave in New England and would have made an example of [Dole] had he not been persuaded by some friends." Dole replied, "Captain, do not threaten me, neither to my face nor behind my back." Henry Greenland then came to his friend's rescue, and Sesegenaway made a hasty exit. Barefoot told Dole to

Interior of Swett-Ilsley House, circa 1670, formerly the Swett tavern. This structure was built just after the notorious Barefoot/Greenland brawl. *HABS photograph.*

get out or he would throw a pot at his head. The next thing Richard Dole remembered, "he threw the pot and struck me on the head backward to the ground, and as soon as I had recovered myself, Mr. Greenland with his hand and foot struck me down backward and trod upon me or kicked me."

Another man, William Thomas, seeing that Richard Dole was in trouble, raced to his defense, but Greenland threw him down and beat him so badly that he was "all bloody, except his eyes," while Barefoot stood at the door to the room, sword drawn, to keep any other patron from helping him. Once Greenland was through with the beating, he "tore [Thomas's coat] in small pieces and then went out of the room," boasting to the other patrons of how he had beaten Dole and Thomas.

Greenland and Barefoot made it as far as the ferry to Salisbury before they were apprehended, but Barefoot put up a good fight. The constable, William Chandler, told the court that it had taken "myself and two to assist me. He would not come on foot, therefore I was constrained to hire four horses, also it was late in the day when I took him."[45] Barefoot escaped from the constable, who found him the next day. The constable also mentioned the difficult time he had finding Dr. Greenland. Finally, the two had their day in court and were fined five pounds each for the brawl and for resisting arrest. Greenland was banished from Essex County and settled in Kittery, and his cantankerous exploits in Newbury ended.

THE SWETT-ILSLEY HOUSE, BUILT 1670, NEWBURYPORT, MASSACHUSETTS 2061

Swett-Ilsley House, circa 1670. The oldest portion of the house is to the left and was known as Swett's, then March's, tavern. *Courtesy of the Historical Society of Old Newbury.*

There were at least three places to buy liquor in Newbury in 1664. Steven Swett's tavern was close to the meetinghouse, near where the Swett-Ilsley House now stands on High Road. Captain Paul White, who had built Newbury's first wharf, was licensed in 1662 to run a distillery and sell "strong waters" by the quart. It is also likely that the first tavern run by Tristram and Dionis Coffin was still in business five years after their departure. By 1668, however, it seems that both taverns had closed down, and the selectmen petitioned the court in Salem "that Captain White be licensed to sell wine out of doors by retail for the necessary relief of some sick or other indigent persons…(and) may also more conveniently accommodate the church's occasions from time to time." Wine was considered medicinal and also necessary to the operations of the church.

CHAPTER 12

Schism

Woodman v. Parker, 1665–1675

Mr. John Woodbridge was an intruder, brought in by craft and subtilty, and so kept in,
notwithstanding he was voated out twice.
—Newbury petition to the Essex County quarterly court, March 30, 1669[46]

John Woodbridge came to Newbury with his uncle, Reverend Thomas Parker, and first did service to the town as clerk from 1635 to 1638. He left in 1639 to marry Mercy Dudley, the governor's daughter, and preached in Andover until returning to England in 1647. It is not clear what induced him to return to Newbury sixteen years later, in 1663. James Noyes, the well-loved co-preacher and companion of Reverend Parker, had died seven years before, and Parker had carried on without interruption on his own. It is possible that, given his uncle's advancing age (he was sixty-eight in 1663), Woodbridge had been summoned by his uncle in order to assist him. It is also possible that he requested a placement in his old hometown. Whatever the case, upon his arrival in Newbury, he was offered thirty pounds for the half year remaining and was put to work. Almost immediately, trouble began.

In 1664, when it came time to renew his contract, Woodbridge was offered sixty pounds, and his uncle's salary was reduced from eighty pounds to sixty. This arrangement lasted for one year and was perceived by supporters of Reverend Parker as an insult. He had, after all, been the founder of the church in Newbury and was its faithful minister for thirty years; Woodbridge had upset the delicate balance that existed between Parker and his parishioners. In 1665, the town voted to raise Reverend Parker's salary to eighty pounds once again, and to keep Woodbridge at sixty. Immediately, a motion was made to eliminate Woodbridge's salary, and when it was again put to a vote, the town returned four votes in the affirmative and thirty-one blank. Woodbridge got his money in 1665, despite protest, but every year thereafter there was a struggle over it, until he was finally let go in 1670. There were, however, enough residents who saw him as a leader that, when they migrated to New Jersey in 1665, they named their town after him. Perhaps it was the core of his supporters who left town, leaving him exposed to his enemies.

Though there had been rumblings of dissatisfaction with Reverend Parker before Woodbridge returned, his arrival seems to have brought matters to a head. The core complaint against them both was that they were not true Congregationalists; that is, they did not submit to the authority of the congregation as a whole. Though Parker respected the opinions of the members of the church, he felt that ultimately it was up to him to accept or reject new members, to allow members to speak in meeting and to ban any members from the meetinghouse.

The root of this trouble began, ironically, with Reverend James Noyes, who seems to have been a man of such personal charm that his negative feelings toward Congregationalism never caused him any trouble. In 1647, Noyes published a book in England laying out his reasons for not recognizing the authority of the congregation:

> The church [i.e., the congregation] is to be carried, not to carry; to obey, not to command; to be subject, not to govern…It is work enough, a double labor, for the elders to instruct the church how to judge…Must elders hold the hands of common members (as a master teaches scholars to write), and act only by them?

The result of such an approach, he said, would be "confusion and disorder."[47]

Most Puritan churches at that time believed strictly in the power of congregational self-government, and though Reverend Parker was a well-loved and well-respected member of the community, he was facing a new generation of church members, the sons of the men who had accompanied him on his journey to Newbury from England. With the addition of John Woodbridge, whose salary they resented and whose personality seems to have been perceived as haughty and overbearing, the issue of church government led to all-out war within the Newbury church. Since the town's church records prior to 1674 have been destroyed or lost, it is in the county court records that the first accusations can be found.

THE WOODMAN FACTION

Edward Woodman was part of the group who had arrived with Parker, and he and John Woodbridge had served together as young men in the 1630s as representatives to the General Court. He had been a commissioner of small causes, a selectman and one of only fifteen of the first settlers of Newbury with high enough social status to have earned the official title "Mr." It must have come as a bit of a shock, therefore, when he stood up in a public assembly on March 1, 1669, and denounced John Woodbridge as "an intruder, brought in by craft and subtlety, and so kept in, notwithstanding he was voted out twice."

Many members of the congregation were outraged, and a petition was immediately dispatched to the county court, claiming that Woodman had

> said to Mr. Parker that he was an apostate and backslider from the truth, and that he would set up a prelacy and have more power than the pope…that his practice did not tend to peace or salvation, and that he was the cause of all our contention and misery.[48]

Three weeks later, Reverend Parker put the question of Woodbridge's employment to the church by asking those who wished him to go to speak up and those who wished him to stay to be silent. Parker decided that more people were silent, and therefore Woodbridge should stay.

The court was not pleased with Edward Woodman's outburst, judging many of his statements regarding Parker and Woodbridge to have been "false and scandalous,…and the whole greatly offensive." Woodman was sentenced to be "seriously and solemnly admonished and enjoined to make a public confession…of his sinful expressions."[49]

It is telling of the complexity of the situation, which involved conflicting interpretations of the votes by which Woodbridge had been retained, that two judges in the case issued dissenting opinions. They offered a very different interpretation, acknowledging that Woodman's words "are highly offensive and scandalous," but then stated that his frustration was understandable, since a large number of the congregation disagreed with Reverend Parker's heavy-handed government, and "it has been for a long time a great burden and grievance to them." These two judges recommended that *both* sides, including Edward Woodman, should publicly confess "their errors and miscarriages and actings…in their public agitations."

Although they won the case, Reverend Parker's supporters' sense of injury was carried forward by these minority opinions, and they shot off a long letter of protest to the court. They accused the dissenting judges of "infamous libels," blaming the trouble in the church entirely on Edward Woodman and his band of supporters and insinuating that it was his rabble-rousing that had turned Parker away from the congregational form of government in the first place, Mr. Woodman being "the chief instrument to oppose the minister."

The court was divided along the same lines as Newbury itself. Edward Woodman had the support of no less than the venerable Richard Dummer, whose first break with the church had come in 1637, when he was disarmed for his heretical tendencies. The redoubtable John Emery, who had had words with Parker over the Quaker women, also supported Woodman, as did the one-time tavern keeper Stephen Swett. Among Reverend Parker's principal supporters were Tristram Coffin Jr., Captain William Gerrish and Richard Dole. The townspeople quickly took one side or the other, and the war of words began.

Since the court could not solve the problem legally, it summoned a council of churches to convene in Newbury and settle the conflict. This council produced its report in November 1669 and declared that Woodman and his friends were entirely in the wrong, having deviated "from the rules of gospel order" by setting up their own church councils, making members of the congregation answer to them "for matters offensive to them" and "undermining and destroying gospel order and peace." They did not censure Woodman, however, but asked the group to look for a compromise, encouraging Parker to "find a way to use all gaining and winning means…that they with their dissenting brethren may become one in the Lord as in former times." The council closed with these hopeful words: "And now reverend and dear brethren, we commend you to God and the word of his grace…and the Lord of peace himself give you peace always by all means. The Lord be with you all."

Far from bringing peace to Newbury, the decision of the council seemed to inflame matters further. By May 1670, the town was so torn that it found it impossible to form a military company as required by the colony, and "for the better composure and prevention of the increase [of infighting] thereof, Major General Leverett and Major Dennison are empowered to inquire into the grounds thereof on the spot, and settle it if possible." Where the county court and a church convention had failed, the military officers succeeded, at least in convincing the town that, for its own safety, they needed to work together. Archelaus Woodman, Edward Woodman's brother, was made lieutenant, and another Woodman supporter, Stephen Greenleaf, was made ensign. They were both eventually put under the command of a Reverend Parker supporter, Daniel Peirce Jr.

STALEMATE

The fight in the meetinghouse raged on, however. On February 13, 1670, John Webster, husband of Betty Webster and John Emery's son-in-law, read a paper in a public meeting condemning Reverend Parker and claiming that opponents of Parker and John Woodbridge now constituted the majority of the congregation.

> *You seem to lay the major part of the church under a censure and to deny any further treating with them until they have reconciled themselves to their offended brethren by confessing such faults as you have charged upon them. To these things thus charged upon us, the major part of the brethren adhering to Jesus Christ and his word do answer, that we do not judge ourselves guilty of those sins as you have publicly charged upon us.*

Far from playing the role of peacemaker, Reverend Parker had suspended conversations with the men who had initially expressed their dissatisfaction with him. Hauled into court, John Webster was found guilty of libel, but he does not seem to have been punished since he was expressing the opinion of other men as well. John Woodbridge's salary was not approved in 1670, but he stayed on in town, and his departure from the ministry did nothing to calm the church.

On March 16, 1670, Woodman and his supporters sent a letter to Reverend Parker, claiming the authority to force him to step down:

> [We] *having seriously considered of the complaint brought to us by Mr. Woodman against our reverend pastor, master Parker, and do judge it clearly proved by sufficient evidences, and much of it known to ourselves to be true, do judge that you have been instrumental of the divisions and troubles, that have a long time [been] and still are, continued in this church, partly by your change of opinion and practice and several times breaking promises and covenants or agreements with the church, and other things*

contained in the complaint, therefore we cannot but judge you worthy of blame, and do hereby blame you, and for the restoring of peace to the church we are enforced, though with great grief of heart, to suspend you from acting any thing that doth appertain to your office, in administering seals and sacraments, or matters of government as an officer, until you have given the church satisfaction therewith.[50]

The first signature on this letter is Richard Dummer, who also let it be known that he and Edward Woodman had been elected "ruling elders" and that they would be ordained a week later. Forty-one prominent members of the church signed this letter, "laying Mr. Parker under blame, and suspending him from all official acts in the church."[51]

Reverend Parker was quick to respond:

Do not think it a light matter to break the unity and peace of the church, hinder the edification of the church, cast contempt on the ministry, grieve your pastor and brethren, give offence to other churches, and bring up an evil report and cast reproach upon the government of the churches here, and once more I entreat you to think of some way of reconciling our differences, which we think will only be by consenting with us to call a regular council, resolving to submit to their advice. If we cannot prevail with you by this motion, we shall be forced to consider what courses shall be taken to defend ourselves, and blame us not for using any lawful means whereby we redress your sin and our distractions.

Parker was not afraid to threaten legal proceedings against the wayward sheep in his flock, and Edward Woodman, whose appearances at court were beginning to prove costly, seemed almost conciliatory in his return letter:

We thought good to put you in mind how far it is from the rule of Christian love so to practice one against another before court and county, which might be healed at home with a word of reproof from one brother to another.

To no one's surprise, the tenacious Reverend Parker did not step down. He immediately had a letter drawn up by his own supporters, denouncing Woodman and Dummer's attempt to become ruling elders and ending communion with them:

We do hereby declare that for the future we do renounce communion with all those brethren that have so deeply violated the communion of Christ's church, nor shall we accept them as regular members of the church of Christ among us till God shall give them a mind to see and heart to acknowledge and confess their great offences.

The Newbury church was at a stalemate. Edward Woodman and his party had withdrawn from the rest of the congregation and declared themselves the true church, denying the authority of Reverend Parker, who, for his part, had ended all communication with them. In April 1670, the council of churches was again called in to examine the matter, but not before Edward Woodman fired off a long letter to them, alternately angry ("we had no hand in your call") and conciliatory ("we do heartily wish that God would make instruments for the settlement of peace and truth amongst us"). The council replied that it would be sure to hear Woodman's side of the disagreement when it examined the case. On the afternoon of April 19, Reverend Parker's charges against Woodman and his party were read aloud, followed by Woodman's twenty-six charges against Parker. Four days later, Woodman's party submitted an additional charge.

A New Covenant

The council spent three days in discussion with all the parties involved, and on April 22, it released a copy of a new covenant, the document that was to be the basis of all future church dealings in Newbury and Newbury's first formal church agreement. It was central to the debate that Newbury had been without a covenant, since the church was first convened outside, under a tree, and those present had different recollections of what Parker had promised.

The new covenant seemed to be a vindication at last of Edward Woodman and his Congregationalist beliefs. It begins with a reiteration of the church's belief in the congregational form of government.

> First, that the platform of discipline, established by the General Court, practiced by the churches of New England, shall be the rule or standard of the congregational way according to which the church of Newbury do resolve both pastor and brethren to act in all church administrations.

This meant that any issue that could not be resolved between the minister and elders of the church directly would have to be brought before the entire congregation for a vote. They advised a waiting period of two weeks for new members, so that the minister and elders would have a chance to discuss their admission. The covenant was signed by Woodman and Dummer, and it brought them back into the church for a year.

At the April 1671 session of the quarterly courts, an exasperated group of parishioners brought a petition against Woodman and his party, charging that they had repeatedly shown "contemptuous behavior" toward the minister during the previous months. They reminded the court of the law that "every person, that shall revile the person or office of magistrates, or ministers, such person or persons shall be severely whipped or pay the fine of five pounds" and suggested that it was about time that someone whipped Edward Woodman. They charged that Woodman's followers "have irregularly convened, have publicly read and debated certain articles presented to them by Mr. Edward Woodman against our pastor, Mr. Parker, whose inoffensiveness is generally known."

Woodman and Parker were having regular shouting matches in the meetinghouse, each accusing the other of breaking his covenant. After Parker was finished with the service, Woodman would get up and begin speaking to the crowd about the minister's false beliefs, and on several occasions, Woodman broke in and rang the bell to call a meeting, sending the confused townsfolk rushing to the meetinghouse. The petitioners begged the court to intervene, reminding it that their salvation depended on it.

Woodman immediately fired off a response, defending his right to challenge the minister and asserting that, by law, two elders could call a meeting if they wished. He also suggested that Parker's followers should be the ones punished by the court, for the reason that it was libelous to bring the complaint against him in the first place. John Woodbridge wrote a lengthy defense of his uncle to the court, accusing Edward Woodman of "bringing forth a monstrous birth" by trying to set up his own church. These were high words indeed, as "monstrous births" were most often associated with witchcraft or evil.

Edward Woodman took off with the church book of records and refused to give it back. Town government ground to a halt, the military companies collapsed and neighbors traded insults in the street. The court responded severely this time, saying it was

> sensibile of the dishonor to the name of God, to religion here established and also the disturbance of the peace, [and] the scandalizing of a venerable, loving and pious pastor and an aged father [and therefore] can not but judge the said Woodman, Mr. Dummer, and William Titcomb. [and] the parties joining with them guilty of very great misdemeanors.

Woodman and his followers were fined and warned that they would be punished even more harshly if they did not make peace with the rest of the congregation.

Meanwhile, Woodman and Dummer looked to the town that had, in the past, most often accepted disgruntled Newbury churchgoers: Rowley. In February 1671, Woodman's brother sent a letter to the Rowley minister, Samuel Phillips, asking him to support their cause and meet them at the tavern at the end of the month to give them advice. They also suggested that Salisbury might want to get involved. Phillips brought the letter to the Rowley congregation. The answer was immediate and clear: "A covenant breaker is very hardly set, and if nine churches could hardly be instrumental of your peace, how you think two should set you at rights we cannot easily imagine." Without the agreement of Reverend Parker to such an intervention, Rowley would not get involved.

Woodman's group was persistent, however, and sent another letter to Rowley, this time asking for Reverend Phillips to preach at the ordination of Edward Woodman and Richard Dummer as "ruling elders," an idea that they still pursued. This time, Reverend Phillips was not so polite. "I conceive you are far out of God's way," he said, "nor do I believe that any church in the colony will stand by you."

THE GENERAL COURT WEIGHS IN

The General Court took up the matter in May 1671. Though Woodman, Dummer and the majority of their followers had been heavily fined, it had done nothing to heal the rift in the church. The General Court recommended that representatives from the churches of Dedham, Charlestown, Boston and Roxbury be sent to Newbury, "that they may enquire into their state and offer them their best advice."[52] A letter was dispatched to Reverend Parker to let the congregation know that help was on the way. The minister and his flock were also challenged to consider the "doleful and deplorable condition" their church was in and to be ready to "humble yourselves greatly before the Lord, to beg that pardon of God…without which there can never be healing amongst yourselves." The council spent a year meeting with the congregation and the dissenters, and while they were reporting back to the General Court, John Woodbridge stepped back into the fray.

Woodbridge had not been a paid minister in the Newbury church for two years in January 1672, but that did not stop him from involving himself in the church conflict once again and rousing the indignation of the patient Rowley minister, Samuel Phillips. Woodbridge overheard that Reverend Phillips had been speaking with Woodman's party, particularly that Phillips had criticized Reverend Parker for continuing to offer communion when there were so many former members of his congregation no longer included. Woodbridge fired off an angry letter to Phillips, accusing him of taking Woodman's side.

Phillips was outraged, for he had refused to support Woodman, and now he laid into Woodbridge and Reverend Parker for what he perceived to be their unapologetic heavy-handedness with their congregation. He accused Parker of refusing admittance to qualified members, not following the new covenant made with the first council of churches, and not having sufficient patience with Woodman and his followers. Woodbridge answered his letter, accusing Phillips of admitting Newbury church members to communion in Rowley and calling him a "busy-body."

The council of churches gave its report to the General Court in May 1672, once again finding fault with both parties, but making a special point of telling John Woodbridge to back off. "We desire, request and advise the reverend Mr. Woodbridge, not to impose himself or his ministry (however otherwise desirable) upon this church." They recommended that Reverend Parker, considering his "great age and weakness…and thereby his unfitness to manage church discipline," accept the assistance of one or two elders.

Later that year, the General Court set up a council whose sole purpose was to make the church behave and report violations to the Court. In the end, it was only the presence of eight "peacekeepers" and the decline in Reverend Parker's health that allowed the church to function. By 1674, Reverend Parker was completely blind and had lost his ability to speak, most likely the result of a stroke. Nicholas Noyes, the son of Parker's cousin and co-minister James Noyes, described his condition as "palsy of the tongue," which allowed him to communicate with others not in words, but with individual letters, spelling out his thoughts, "which was indeed a tedious way."[53] He was replaced officially in 1675 by Reverend John Richardson, who had been hired to assist him. When Thomas Parker died in 1677, despite his controversial final years he was still a respected member of his community, and the river by whose banks he first gathered his church was named after him in 1697.

CHAPTER 13

KING PHILIP'S WAR AND
ITS AFTERMATH

I Daniell Sumerby beeing Caled to goe forth to war by gods prouidens: this is my will that my sister
Elizabeths Clarkes eldest soon shall bee my Ayre of all my Lands.
—*Will of Daniel Somerby, Oct. 26, 1675*[54]

Reverend Parker lived long enough to experience the crisis that turned everyone's attention away from squabbles in the meetinghouse. In 1675, the brittle peace with the native tribes in the colony was shattered. Three native men were hanged in Plymouth Colony in June for the murder of a Christian "praying Indian," who had warned the colonists of an impending attack. Tribal groups led by the Wampanoag sachem Metacomet, known to the English colonists as King Philip, began to attack and burn frontier settlements throughout Plymouth and Massachusetts Bay Colonies.

Newbury men were formed in organized, commissioned military companies, and all healthy men were expected to be trained and armed. With the outbreak of war, they were drafted into service and organized into special companies, often with men from other towns. Beginning in August 1675, Newbury men, horses, supplies and ammunition were sent into the conflict in increasing numbers. Most of the men pressed into service in August 1675 were sent out not to fight, but to harvest the crops of settlers who had fled their homes and were now in danger of starving.

In September 1675, the Essex County regiment was returning from threshing wheat in Deerfield when it was ambushed, and most of the men were killed or wounded, including many from Newbury. As word trickled back from the frontier of houses burned, crops destroyed and settlers murdered, those left home in Newbury began to fear being burned in their beds. Even the venerable Reverend Parker, who had seen a half century of planning and worrying about Indians attacking, was filled with dread, as related a quarter century later by his fellow Puritan minister Cotton Mather:

> *During that time, which was in our first Indian war, when the Indians broke in upon many towns, and committed horrible outrages, and tormented such as they took captives, one night he fell into a dreadful temptation, lest the Indians should break in upon Newbury, and the inhabitants might generally escape by fighting or flying, but he being old and blind, and grown decrepit, he must of necessity fall into their hands; and that*

being a minister, they would urge him by torture to blaspheme Christ, and that he should not have grace to hold out against the temptation of Indian torture; and with the very fear of this, he was for the most part of the night in such agonies of soul, that he was on the very brink of desperation.[55]

While Reverend Parker lay in his bed terrified of being captured and tortured, the congregation that he had recently left fortified the meetinghouse with two seven- to eight-hundred-pound cannons, and Newbury men fought and died in the defense of Hadley, Deerfield and Springfield.

In December 1675, a group of twenty-six Newbury men gathered for a final attack on a Narragansett fort in Connecticut. The fort had been built in a swamp, making it nearly impossible to attack until the ground was frozen. It was winter and snowing hard, and after marching for days and camping outside, the exhausted soldiers finally led the assault on December 16. Four Newbury men were killed and five wounded. Among the wounded was Daniel Somerby, the twenty-five-year-old stepson of Tristram Coffin Jr. Somerby returned home, but the wound claimed his life in March 1676.

Just after Somerby's death, the town of Newbury voted to fortify the community: "We have ordered several houses to be garrisoned and fortified and men appointed and are about fortifying with a mile or somewhat more from river to river most of our plow lands and houses." The attack on the Narragansett swamp fort proved to be a turning point in the war, but raids on outlying towns continued, even after the death of Metacomet in August 1676. From the first call-up to the last during King Philip's War, sixty-eight men and forty-six horses from Newbury were drafted for military service—fully half the men in the town served at some point. There were a few years of quiet in Newbury after the end of King Philip's War, but tensions with the natives would flare again at the end of the century.

DOMESTIC AFFAIRS

Reverend Parker lived long enough after the war to hear of one more outrageous scuffle in the meetinghouse. On March 27, 1677, at the county court session in Salem, "Joshua Richardson, Caleb Richardson, and Edward Ordway were sentenced to be severely whipped or pay a fine of ten pounds each, for breaking into the meetinghouse, demolishing pew chairs and so forth." The selectmen had given several women permission to build a new seat in the corner of the gallery, and whether out of personal spite or involvement in a family dispute, at least three young men broke into the meetinghouse by smashing the windows and destroyed the new seat. Prominent members of the town petitioned to have their fines reduced, since the new seats were not acceptable to many members of the congregation, and the town voted not to allow the women to rebuild them. One month later, secure at least in the knowledge that he was not the sole cause of unrest in the Newbury congregation, Reverend Parker died at the house he had shared with James and Sarah Noyes and their children for over forty years.

One of the many valuable services that Reverend Parker provided during his lifetime was the preparation of exceptional students to attend Harvard. Though there had been a grammar school as early as 1639, it was particularly difficult to keep schoolmasters employed. Since their pay came primarily from the students' parents, it was an unreliable income, and the work was difficult. As early as 1652, there was something like a school board set up "for managing the business of the school," and the town voted to pay a schoolmaster in part from town taxes. In 1658, however, Newbury was fined for not having an appropriate school and was ordered to pay Ipswich for the education of its children.

In 1676, the town appointed Henry Short to keep school for a year and allowed him the use of the "watch house." Though there are no records of where the watch house stood, or indeed what it looked like, it was probably not part of the "watch" set up on Old Town Hill, as that location was then far from the center of town. The watch house appears in the town records first as a place where school was taught and later as a jail,

Rear ell of James Noyes House, where Thomas Parker lived until his death in 1677. Photograph by Arthur C. Haskell. *Courtesy of Historic New England.*

Front door of the Henry Short House. *HABS photograph.*

and it was probably set up somewhere close to the meetinghouse. Henry Short declined the use of the building, however, and taught seventeen students at his house. This arrangement apparently did not suit him, and the following year Newbury was again hunting for a schoolmaster. All along, Reverend Parker tutored students in Latin and Greek, and many young men from Newbury attended Harvard.

In 1678, a year after Reverend Parker's death, John Woodbridge surfaced again, this time as the administrator of an oath of allegiance to the king to all men over the age of sixteen. In all, 236 men took the oath, meaning there were probably close to 600 men, women and children living in the town. Perhaps unsurprisingly, Woodbridge would also have a key role to play in the next scandal that shook the town. When he had first returned from England in 1663, he stirred up tensions in the meetinghouse; in 1679, he turned his considerable energy to witch hunting.

CHAPTER 14

THE WITCH AND THE WIZARD, 1679

A mate of A ship Coming often to me and said he much grefed for me and said the boye was the case of all my truble and my wife was much Ronged, and was no wich, and if I would let him have the boye but one day he would warrant me no more truble. I being persuaded to it he Com the nex day at the brek of day, and the boy was with him untel night and I had not any truble since.
—Testimony of William Morse, December 6, 1679[56]

At age sixty-five, William Morse was considered an old man in 1679. He had been one of the original settlers in 1635, and he spent some time as a shepherd for the town and also as a shoemaker. He had been granted four acres of land near Watt's Cellar in exchange for relinquishing his house lot in the old town, and he built a house on this property. In 1679, he lived there with his wife, Elizabeth, and their grandson. Both William and Elizabeth Morse were members of the Newbury church, and William Morse had been one of the men who had brought Edward Woodman and his followers to court for usurping the authority of Reverend Parker and John Woodbridge. Both William and Elizabeth could read and write. They had taken in their grandson, John Stiles, whose mother was their daughter Hannah.

The Morse family was an odd, fragmented bunch. Not only is there no record of John Stiles's father, but the Morses also had another grandchild born out of wedlock to their daughter Abigail, and their two sons, Jonathan and Obadiah, moved away from Newbury as young men and did not return. How John Stiles came to live with them is a mystery, as his mother, Hannah, was still living when William Morse died. What is certain is that, whatever his background, John Stiles was a very troubled boy.

In November 1679, William and Elizabeth Morse were asleep in their house when they heard "a great noise" outside the house. They went outside to see what was making the noise and were hit with a barrage of sticks and stones. After returning to bed, they heard another loud sound, this time on the roof, and were awakened at midnight by the sound of a huge hog loose in the kitchen. They let the hog out and noticed that the door was unlocked, but returned to their beds.

The next morning, the disturbances began again in earnest. Stones, tools and baskets clattered down the chimney. Pots seemed to dump themselves out. Spoons flew off the table, barrels exploded and William Morse's pen and ink disappeared.

Water pump at Market Square. The Morse house was on the left (south) side of State Street, but its exact location is unknown. Photograph by George E. Noyes. *Courtesy of Historic New England.*

He was hit in the head with shoes, ears of corn, stones and sticks, and Elizabeth's hat was knocked off her head. Another hog was loose in the kitchen. When William sent his grandson out to check on their cows, a shed collapsed on the boy. A chair seemed to bow to him.

Word quickly spread through the town of this activity, and eventually it came to the attention of Caleb Powell, a ship's mate temporarily living in Newbury. William and Elizabeth were desperate for relief from their seemingly supernatural affliction, and Caleb Powell offered it to them. They may also have been afraid that Elizabeth would be accused of witchcraft and were happy for his help in clearing her name. He had studied astronomy, astrology and "the working of the spirits." One of his shipmates declared that "if there were any wizards, he was sure Caleb Powell was one." Whatever his powers, Powell offered to rid the Morse household of its enchantment, since he was "much grieved" for them.

He had immediately identified the cause of their problems, and his solution was to remove John Stiles from the Morse house. Powell came to the house on one occasion, and seeing that William Morse was praying, he waited outside and watched through the window as John Stiles threw shoes and other objects at his grandfather. Powell quickly confronted him, according to Morse, and *said the boy was the cause of all my trouble…and if I would let him have the boy but one day he would warrant me no more trouble. I being persuaded to it he came the next day at the break of day, and the boy was with him until night and I had not any trouble since.*

With Stiles dealt with, the activity immediately stopped, but Powell's involvement almost cost him his life. William Morse, unwilling to believe that his grandson had been the cause of their troubles, brought Caleb Powell to court in December 1679. He testified that since Powell was the one to remove the curse, he must have been the wizard who inflicted it. With Powell locked up awaiting trial, the afflictions began again, this time seeming to affect John Stiles most of all. He began to suffer "fits" and "afflictions." He fell into the fire and complained constantly of being pricked and stabbed. He barked like a dog and clucked like a chicken. Each time, he identified Powell as his tormentor, pinching him or spiriting him away to fly over the town at night.

If Powell had taken Stiles away and told him to knock off the nonsense, it certainly backfired. With Powell in jail and the Morses convinced that he was the cause of their trouble, Stiles was free to abuse them and implicate Powell. Even though the activity stopped on the two occasions that Stiles was taken to a doctor, the blame was pinned squarely on Powell. The court heard the case against him in January 1680 and came to an ambiguous conclusion:

> *Upon hearing the complaint brought to this court against Caleb Powell for suspicion of working by the devil to the molesting of the family of William Morse of Newbury, though this court cannot find any evident ground of proceeding farther against the said Powell, yet we determine that he hath given such ground of suspicion of his so dealing that we cannot so acquit him but that he justly deserves to bear his own shame and the costs of prosecution of the complaint.*[57]

Caleb Powell was not guilty of witchcraft, but it seemed that he was probably guilty of scamming the Morse family out of some money, and both his status as an unattached sailor and his claims of occult powers made him highly suspect. Still, upon payment of court costs, he was released.

The good citizens of Newbury do not seem to have been willing to let it go at that, however. The Morse household was too strange and the devilry too extreme to be the actions of one troubled boy. The neighbors started to talk about their odd encounters with Elizabeth Morse, and John Woodbridge began gathering testimony against the wife of his old ally in the meetinghouse. It did not take long before Elizabeth Morse's neighbors were remembering small insults and slights from decades before.

By March, a warrant was sworn out for Elizabeth Morse, and she was taken by the Newbury constable to the Ipswich jail. Also in March, Caleb Powell was released, and he certainly would have had a motive for stirring up the townspeople against his accusers. In April, Woodbridge gathered more depositions, and by May, Elizabeth Morse had been transferred to Boston to await her grand jury trial for witchcraft. Seventeen people accused Elizabeth Morse of witchcraft, for crimes as varied as sickening cattle and turning into a cat. One neighbor accused her of knowing what was inside a sealed envelope. Another testified that when she nailed a horseshoe to her door, Elizabeth Morse would not come in her house.

Almost all of the testimony against her involved a quarrel or sharp words of some kind, and they had all taken place years before. Elizabeth Morse was not afraid to tell people what she thought of them. She also seems to have been a healer or midwife, present at the birth and death of family members, and she was a suspect when things did not go as planned. Four of her accusers complained that she had caused them physical harm, from sore breasts to "bloody flux." When babies died in her care, she was blamed. Several accusers mentioned her visits to the sickbeds of their parents or children. Calves, lambs and horses all had sickened and died after their owners had argued with Elizabeth Morse.

A committee of women was summoned to examine her body for marks of the devil, and her Newbury neighbors arrived in Boston to swear to their testimony against her. On May 27, 1680, Elizabeth Morse was found guilty of witchcraft, and her sentence was read by the governor:

> *Elizabeth Morse, you are to go from hence to the place from whence you came and thence to the place of execution and there to be hanged by the neck, till you be dead, and the Lord have mercy on your soul.*

It was not so simple to hang Elizabeth Morse, however. Several members of the court disagreed with the sentence, and though they were not able to overturn it, they succeeded in delaying her execution until October. She suffered through a sweltering summer in the Boston Jail. William sent repeated requests that she be allowed to walk outside in the daytime, housed in the regular jail rather than in the dungeon and allowed to attend church. During the fall session, her execution was once again delayed. The representatives responsible for her sentence protested this delay.

Still, she was reprieved again until May 1681, when her husband sent two lengthy petitions to the court refuting the charges against her. One of these petitions was written out and delivered by the same Lieutenant Pike of Salisbury, whose petition against organized preaching had been signed by William Morse back in 1653. In 1681, William came out in force, replying to his wife's accusers with deft logic. If there had been so many instances when she had shown herself to be a witch, why had she not been censured by the church? Why were her friends and neighbors accusing her after years had gone by and she could not remember an alleged slight and defend herself?

Elizabeth petitioned for another hearing, but the court again delayed, this time sending her home, but still under penalty of death. Once released from jail, the court declined to proceed further, and Elizabeth Morse spent the rest of her life in her house in Newbury, allowed to leave only to go to the meetinghouse. It was a narrow, almost inexplicable escape for her; just a decade later, on even flimsier evidence than that used against Elizabeth Morse, nineteen women would be hanged in Salem for witchcraft.

CHAPTER 15

THE PORT, PLUM ISLAND AND THE POOR

The proprietors of Ipswich...finding themselves much damnified in that their marshes were trodden to dirt and almost utterly spoiled by a multitude of horses and other cattle put thereon by those of Newbury in the winter, to live of what they can get and suffered there to continue till the middle of May, if not longer.
—Ipswich selectmen to the General Court, May 28, 1679[58]

It was in the late 1670s that Newbury's residents seem to have finally begun putting their prime waterside location to good use. Captain Paul White had been granted a half acre in 1655 to build a dock and a wharf, and in 1677, Richard Dole asked for permission to build a dock "about Watts his cellar" as well. He was given permission and granted the necessary land, with the understanding that "all boats belonging to the town shall have free liberty...to lie there as occasion may serve." The town also granted him the land "which is commonly known as Captain White's point."

Captain White was eighty-six years old in 1677, and Richard Dole's wharf and dock probably replaced his. White had not enjoyed great profit from his relationship with the town, complaining that he had been overtaxed by the town and that whatever he made as a shopkeeper and trader was already taxed by the colony:

> *If any object that my gains by shop keeping is considerable; I do here affirm, (and shall readily take my oath to it being called thereto) that I have not sold fifty pounds worth of goods this twelve months...besides I pay a penny in ye pound for all my goods as soon as they come ashore.*

In addition, he had no land, and therefore, "I am fain to buy every stick of wood I burn, every inch of timber I use." Paul White's appearance in the court records also reveals that he had business dealings in Barbados and that he owned a slave.

In 1679, Daniel Davison was also given permission to make a shipbuilding dock around Watt's Cellar. Aside from this coveted spot by Watt's Cellar, today the heart of downtown Newburyport, there was also a shipbuilding enterprise at the foot of Kent Street, run by the enterprising son of Edward Woodman. In 1678, Jonathan Woodman had completed work on a ship called the *Salamander*, and he went to court with the

View of the waterfront, late nineteenth century. The earliest docks and wharves were clustered around Watt's Cellar, in the center of the waterfront in this image. *Courtesy of the Historical Society of Old Newbury.*

prospective owners over how much money was still owed. When he died in 1706, his will identified him as a "shipwright," and he left his son with a load of timber—a valuable gift for the new owner of an active shipyard. It is also likely that George Carr, engaged as he was in the ferry business, made and repaired boats, though there is no mention of a ship being made at Carr Island until the 1690s.

During Elizabeth's trial, right around the corner from the Morse house, the waterfront was booming. Richard Dole's wharf was joined by one that Stephen Greenleaf and Daniel Davison were given permission to build in 1680, "provided the inhabitants of the town shall have liberty to land wood or hay or other goods so that the said goods be not above twenty-four hours, neither at any time to do them damage." Five additional men petitioned the town for permission to build wharves (some of them in company with each other), and they all received permission and an admonishment to be done with their work in three years.

Though the residents of the town were not yet living close to the water, their business ventures increasingly led them to the sea. In 1680, Governor Simon Bradstreet defined Newbury business as "some little trade...for country people." On February 9, 1683, to the chagrin of Newbury's traders, the General Court made Newbury's trade relationship to Salem clear, ordering

> that the port of Boston to which Charlestown is annexed, and the port of Salem, to which Marblehead, Beverly, Gloucester, Ipswich, Rowley, Newbury and Salisbury are annexed, as members, shall be the lawful ports in this colony, where ships and other vessels shall lade or unlade any of the plantation's enumerated goods, or other goods from foreign parts, and nowhere else.

PLUM ISLAND: PASTURE OR TILLAGE?

Newbury had been founded in part as a company that raised livestock, but its early hopes for a quick profit were dashed by a careless herdsman. Still, the marshy meadows and grassy hills of Newbury proved ideal for cattle and sheep, and many families made their living from the animals themselves, or from working with leather and wool. For many years, Plum Island had been a pasture for horses, cattle and hogs. They could be let loose without fear of escape, and marsh grass was plentiful.

By 1679, however, Plum Island was an overcrowded, trampled mess, and animals were often so wild from years of free range that they could not be herded and had to be shot. To make matters worse, rights to the island had been divided between Ipswich, Rowley and Newbury since 1639, and though the town of Newbury repeatedly petitioned the General Court for control of the island, it was only through the sale of individual plots of land that Newbury gradually came into possession of it. By 1679, Newbury and Ipswich men had bought out most of the Rowley share and apparently were at odds as to what to do with it. The Ipswich contingent wanted to be able to grow marsh hay there, while the Newbury proprietors needed pasturage for their animals.

The selectmen of Ipswich petitioned the General Court, protesting the rampant grazing of Newbury livestock, which, they said,

Haystacks and river, Plum Island. Photograph by George E. Noyes. *Courtesy of Historic New England.*

will unavoidably (as experience hath taught us) be the ruin and utter destruction of the whole island, the horses and cattle eating up the grass, that grows upon the sand hills, which gives a stop to the running of the sands in stormy weather, which otherwise would in a very short space cover all the marshes, as we have found at Castle Neck. Wherefore we beseech this honored court to prohibit the putting or going of any horses, cattle and so forth upon the said island.[59]

The General Court answered their petition and ordered "that no horses or cattle be put in said island without the consent of the major part of the proprietors of said island." Though there were only two individual owners of land on Plum Island from Newbury in 1679, Richard Dole and Henry Jaques, the town jealously guarded its citizens' rights of pasturage, and animals continued to roam over Plum Island until the Court finally put a stop to it in 1739. Plum Island was finally sold into private ownership in 1827.[60]

Owners of cattle and horses had two options: they could keep their animals on their own land (clearly the best option for work horses or cows that needed to be milked), or they could send their animals off with the herdsman to graze on common land, but only if they were freeholders and had been granted that right. The largest number of animals made up the "dry herd" of non-milking cattle and untrained horses that were pastured in what is now West Newbury. Though there were constant regulations against it, unauthorized cattle were frequently slipped in with the herd, and the herdsman paid off. If cattle were caught wandering loose, they were impounded, and the constable or hay wardens had the right to sell them or fine their owners.

Though there were several houses on the west side of the Artichoke, the building boom in that area really began in 1686, when the land was divided up into lots both to freeholders and to other members of the church and the town who had not been able to purchase freehold rights. The presence of soldiers returning from King Philip's War also spurred this decision, as many of these young men had no freehold and yet were acknowledged to deserve land. Lots were laid out in the future West Newbury, and within twenty years, over one hundred houses had been built.

Sheep were also a significant source of income for Newbury families. In 1685, there were nearly six thousand sheep in Newbury, divided up into five "sheep walks," each of which had a particular area of the town to graze on and a particular mark, painted in pitch on their hides after they had been shorn. They were not to mix with other flocks "under penalty of twelve pence a head for every sheep so disorderly." The sheep, vulnerable prey animals that they are, were "folded" every night, penned in securely to prevent their being eaten by bear and wolves. This "folding" practice was an enormous benefit to fields in need of fertilization, and the sheep, six to seven hundred at a time, were locked up at night in the fields of various Newbury farmers, where they mulched and manured the soil. Turnips were thought to grow particularly well on land where sheep had been folded and are referred to in the record as "turnip pens." The shepherd was also fed by the family on whose fields the sheep were folded.

WARDS OF THE TOWN

In 1682, a man named Evan Morris was warned out of town, presumably for staying too long without officially appealing to be made a member of the town. He was still around the following year, however, and was made the shepherd, paid a flat fee by the town and also paid by the head by the sheep owners. The town's fears about Evan Morris were justified, however; six years later, the town paid Aquilla Chase "ten shillings per week…but if the said Morris should die within that time, the said Chase shall have proportionally." In other words, the town had let Evan Morris linger too long and was now paying for his care.

Most residents of Newbury relied on the kindness of their extensive family networks in illness or old age, or paid for the services of neighbors who changed sheets and fed the fire, but there were always some who were poor and alone. The care and feeding of the town's destitute members was a constant source of strain, particularly when, in times of flood, drought or pestilence, Newbury's citizens had nothing to spare. If they could be put to work, as Evan Morris was, to provide a service for the town, they were, and the job of shepherd solved the problem of his food as well, since he was both fed and paid by the sheep owners.

John Earles, a man of about seventy, was hired as a farm hand and (perhaps not surprisingly) was unfit for the job. After spending some time looking for work in Newbury and Ipswich, he was sent back to the town in 1644 and ordered to make beehives to help pay for his care. Thomas Turvill was given an acre of land by the selectmen in 1663 to encourage him to make leather. Six years later, however, he was a ward of the town and was sent to live with his relative, Henry Short, "to be maintained at the expense of the town until his death."[61]

Cases like this appear sporadically until the 1680s, when a growing population and port required that a more formalized system be instituted to deal with the poor. In 1682, Newbury voted that the selectmen had the power to provide for the poor and that they could "build a cottage or cottages for them according to their discretion."[62] In 1686, Nicholas Noyes, Tristram Coffin and Robert Long were appointed overseers of the poor, along with Daniel Peirce and Stephen Greenleaf, and any three of them could determine a case for relief. There was no formal poorhouse built in Newbury for another fifty years, and the town's poor were generally kept in private homes at the town's expense. There was certainly a fair amount of private charity as well. When Robert Muzzey died in 1647, he instructed his heirs to "give to the use of the poor one ewe goat to be disposed of by the overseers of my will to such as are godly."

CHAPTER 16

CHURCH AND STATE

The purport of the paper was to give notice to the people of the danger they were in, being under the sad circumstances of an arbitrary government, sir Edmund Andros having about one thousand of our souldiers, as I was informed, prest out of the Massachusetts colony.
—Testimony of Caleb Moody, January 9, 1690[63]

The civil wars in England came to an end in 1661, with Oliver Cromwell's head on a spike and Charles II on the throne. For the first time in decades, the king began to reassert his authority over the colonists. Puritans anywhere were suspect, since the government of Oliver Cromwell was Puritan, and in 1678, an order was sent to the colonies requiring that all males over the age of sixteen take an oath of allegiance to the king. The list from Newbury includes the names and ages of 236 men, and the oath was administered by none other than John Woodbridge. It was an anxious time for the colonists, and they worried, with good cause, that the relative autonomy they had enjoyed during Cromwell's protectorate would be lost.

In 1684, the cross was included in the flag of the Newbury militia, an unthinkable idolatry in the minds of strict Puritans. In that same year, King Charles II revoked the charter of the Massachusetts Bay Colony and lumped it together with other former New England colonies as the Dominion of New England, with Boston as its capital. The citizens of Newbury were confused and alarmed, but business carried on as usual—until the arrival of Sir Edmond Andros, the new governor.

In 1687, Andros settled into Boston and began his tenure as the most hated governor in Massachusetts history. Andros limited the power of the legislature and ordered that towns could hold only one legislative meeting annually. In Newbury, he granted permission for John March to start another ferry, throwing the tenacious Carr family into a frenzy. Town business in Newbury ground to a halt as residents tried to find someone approved by the new governor to serve as town clerk.

There was also a general panic when Andros began pressing soldiers into military service, leaving many towns unguarded and their residents suspecting a plot to remove potential opposition to his government. Newbury's own Caleb Moody was caught with a treasonous document, headed with the verse:

New England alarmed,
To rise and be armed,
Let not papist you charm,
I mean you no harm.

The paper's intent was "to give notice to the people of the danger they were in, being under the sad circumstances of an arbitrary government" that conscripted their best men "under pretence of destroying our enemy Indians."[64] Caleb Moody was thrown in jail, but he was later reprieved and awarded damages.

THE MASON THREAT

Though towns felt undefended and anxious, the most alarming development of all was the new governor's friendship with Robert Mason. Robert Mason was the grandson and heir of John Mason, whose grant of land in 1622 included all the land between the Merrimack and Kennebec Rivers, from Massachusetts into present-day Maine. The same land had been regranted to the colony of Massachusetts Bay, but with the colony's charter revoked, Mason was pressing land claims both north and south of the Merrimack. This raised the fear that all of the land that had been granted to settlers in Newbury would be taken from them and given back to the Mason family, to sell or rent as they pleased.

A petition from the men of Essex County had already gone before the king in 1682, asking for protection from the Mason family claim, since they had lived on their land unmolested until then. Once Robert Mason was on New England soil, however, the citizens of Newbury took a conciliatory approach, courting his favor as he often passed through Newbury on his way to Portsmouth. In August 1687, Mason sent a letter to Governor Andros that erased any doubt about his views on the status of Newbury: "I hope all things will go easy so that I may have no occasion of using the former severities of the law against my tenants. I had rather see them rich than poor."[65] Fortunately for Newbury, Robert Mason died suddenly in 1688, while traveling with Andros, and his sons were not able to press his claim.

Meanwhile, in England, Charles II's brother and successor, James II, who was thought to be Catholic, had produced a son and heir, the beginnings of a potential Catholic dynasty. The country instead turned to his Protestant daughter and son-in-law, William and Mary, who ousted James II in the so-called Glorious Revolution of 1688. When the news of this political realignment reached the colony, Governor Andros was run out of town and attempted escape dressed as a woman, but he was captured and sent to England for trial. William and Mary were more sympathetic to the requests of the colonists, and they reinstated the charter for the province of Massachusetts Bay in 1691.

Though the charter was renewed and Andros ousted, the fate of the Mason grant was still unclear. The 1691 charter specifically stated that it would not interfere with any title held by the Mason family or by Samuel Allen, who had purchased the title from Robert Mason's sons. It is likely that this uncertainty led the people of Newbury to formally purchase their town land from the descendants of Masconomet in 1701, so if pressed they would have additional proof of ownership.

From the restoration of the English monarchy in 1661 to the new colonial charter in 1691, the town of Newbury also took steps to divest itself of much of its common land, since land that had been granted to private individuals was recognized as more difficult for the Mason family to claim. The needs of the town were also changing, as the first freeholders died and their original rights to island, marsh and pasture lots were divided up between numerous children and sold, bartered and fragmented until they became almost impossible to manage. Much of what is now West Newbury was divided up along the Bradford Road, the lower commons were split into five pastures and private woodlots and the narrow strip of land along the banks of the Merrimack River that had not been laid out in 1645 was divided up into river lots in 1708.

The west end of town was booming. John Emery Jr. ran a thriving mill on the Artichoke River, and there were new roads and bridges that finally made it accessible. With the influx of new settlers building in the west end of town came those two pillars of town life: a new tavern, granted to Samuel Sawyer in 1689, and a new meetinghouse, built the same year.

ANOTHER MEETINGHOUSE CONFLICT

The acquisition of a tavern was a simple affair; not so a meetinghouse. The inhabitants of the west end of town first presented a petition to the selectmen, asking that they be granted a minister. Their petition was rejected, and several families made the brazen decision to build a meetinghouse anyway, on "the Plains," from the eastern edge of what is now Maudslay State Park to where Belleville Cemetery now sits on Storey Avenue in Newburyport. In March 1689, they presented the Newbury minister, John Richardson, with a *fait accompli* and a choice: either hire us a second minister and the town can share the cost, or we will form a separate parish and find a minister ourselves.

Richardson, who had managed to heal the bitter religious divides in the community when he had replaced Reverend Parker, was unable to prevent a new conflict. The town of Newbury did not respond favorably once again, and the west end group simply called its own minister: the town's former schoolteacher, Edward Tomson. This was going too far, and the majority of the town censured them by voting that the upstarts' decision was "an intrusion upon the church and the town." Several west end families petitioned the General Court "to be established a people by themselves for the maintenance of the ministry among them."

View of the Merrimack River from Pipestave Hill. The meetinghouse at the Plains would have been in view from here on a clear winter day. Photograph by S.C. Reed. *Courtesy of Historic New England.*

The town took up the challenge, and the fight was on. It voted against the west end plan and chose a committee to present its case to the General Court. The General Court sent a request to the people of Newbury to list the reasons why there should not be a minister appointed for the west end, since there was already a meetinghouse and an acting minister in place. After another year of arguing, the town finally conceded, voting to hire a minister for the west end church. In May 1693, John Clark was "called to assist Mr. Richardson in the work of the ministry at the west end of the town to preach to them one year in order to further settlement and also to keep a grammar school."

Just when it seemed that the west end had gotten its way, another petition went off to the General Court. Apparently, Edward Tomson was still preaching in the west end, not having taken kindly to the move to oust him in favor of John Clark. The west end petitioners pled their case to the Court and begged that they be allowed to choose and support their own minster:

> *The bulk of us live four miles from the old meetinghouse, some six or seven. Our number is above three hundred. Few of us have horses, and if we could get down to the old meetinghouse, it is impossible it should receive us with them, so that many [would] lay out of doors, the house is so little. Some of us have groaned under this burden this thirty years, some grown old…We believe our neighbors would be glad to see us quite tired out. We beg the honorable Court to establish peace among us a rational dividing line.*[66]

Things grew so heated that Newbury resident Joseph Bailey called the men discussing the new minister "devils incarnate."

John Clark stepped out of the fray and declined his appointment as minister, leaving the town to decide between Edward Tomson and Christopher Toppan, a new candidate. The town chose Toppan, and at the end of 1694, at long last, a committee was set up "to draw up articles and proposals in order to setting off part of the west end of the town as a separate parish."

The establishment of a separate parish was a big deal in colonial New England. It meant that the center of social and religious life had shifted. It meant a greater tax burden in both the old parish and the new, since they were supporting two ministers instead of one. When the town grudgingly allowed the west parish to split off, it made one final, fateful pronouncement: though the new meetinghouse would be allowed to stand until the west parish decided to remove or rebuild it, any future meetinghouse was to be much farther away from the center of town, on Pipestave Hill in what is now West Newbury. This mandate was to cause decades of bitter fighting in the west parish, as those who lived closer to the first west parish meetinghouse refused to travel the additional three miles to Pipestave Hill. This conflict would provoke physical altercations, spiritual crisis and a schism in the Puritan church.

But in 1695, as at the end of the last great church conflict in 1675, when King Philip's War erupted, the men, women and children of Newbury faced a more immediate and terrible danger than where to attend meeting. On October 7, the Indian attack the town had feared and prepared for finally happened, and a family was dragged from their Newbury home and killed.

CHAPTER 17

ATTACK, 1695

Sir, this afternoon there came the enemy to a house in our town and went in and took and carried away nine persons and plundered the house, and as near as we can gather, they went southwestwardly between Boxford and Bradford…We have lined Merrimac river with about fourscore men to watch lest they should carry the captives over the river, and do design in the morning to pursue them and range the woods with all the force we can make,…for if they escape us it will be an encouragement to them.
—*Letter from Colonel Daniel Peirce to Colonels Appleton and Wade of Ipswich, October 7, 1695*[67]

Relations with native groups in New England had been strained since the end of King Philip's War in 1676, with the French and their native allies attacking and burning frontier settlements in present-day Maine and New Hampshire. In 1690, Massachusetts Governor William Phips sent an expeditionary force to Port Royal, Nova Scotia, and captured the fort there, beginning a decade of war with the French.

Back in Newbury, the town ordered its men to prepare for attack:

> *All the soldiers belonging to this town* [are ordered] *to bring their arms and ammunition to the meetinghouse every Sabbath day and at all other public meetings, and also they are required to carry their arms and ammunition with them into meadows and places, where they work.*[68]

In February 1692, Richard Dummer's son Shubael, one of the first children born in Newbury and, at the time, the minister in York, Maine, was killed in an Indian attack while mounting his horse, and his wife and children were taken captive. In October 1692, a small native group attacked a family in Georgetown, and there were attacks in Amesbury, Salisbury and Haverhill. Benjamin Pike of Salisbury, who had been defended by so many Newbury men in his youth, had reason again to thank

> *Captain Pierce, Captain Noyes, Captain Greenleaf, and Lieutenant Moore, with the rest of the gentlemen of Newbury, whose assistance next under God was the means of the preservation of our towns of Salisbury and Amesbury in the day of our distress by the assaults of the enemy.*

A guard of thirty soldiers was stationed between Newbury and Bradford.

However, the town's defensive measures proved unable to protect the entire community. On the afternoon of October 7, 1695, John Brown and some other men left their house on Turkey Hill with a load of turnips. Brown left his wife, Ruth, and their six young children at home, likely with their grandmother and other family members. Five or six native men had hidden themselves near the house, and when the men were out of sight, they attacked, killing a young girl and carrying away nine members of the Brown family. One girl managed to avoid capture and immediately raised the alarm.

Colonel Daniel Peirce sent off a hurried message to Ipswich, begging for help in catching the raiding party before they could escape across the Merrimack with their captives:

> We can not gather that there were above five of the enemy, but night came on so that we could not pursue them, but we have lined Merrimac River with about fourscore men to watch lest they should carry the captives over the river, and do design in the morning to pursue them and range the woods with all the force we can make, and think it advisable that you range the woods towards Andover, and that Rowley towards Bradford, for if they escape us it will be an encouragement to them. Sir, I do think the case requires our utmost industry.[69]

Colonel Appleton of Ipswich got the message at 5:00 a.m. on October 8, responded immediately and sent to Salem for additional help, "so that...the enemy may be found and destroyed, which spoil our people." Ipswich turned out in full force, determined that the captives not be carried across the Merrimack River and into the wilderness, where their chances of being rescued would be slim.

As it happened, Ipswich and Salem need not have come at all, as Captain Stephen Greenleaf of Newbury came upon the raiding party and their captives at about 9:00 p.m., hidden in a ditch by the road. In the darkness and confusion that followed, captain Greenleaf was shot through the side and wrist, and the raiders escaped into the woods and across the river. The fate of the captives is uncertain. It seems that, ultimately, they were all rescued, except one, who was killed, and several were certainly wounded. Cotton Mather, in his 1702 *Magnalia Christi Americana*, claimed that they were beaten "so unmercifully that they all afterward died except one lad who was only hurt in the shoulder. Some of them lingered for six months, and some for more than a year, suffering from their wounds."

The following year, Captain Greenleaf, permanently disabled from his wounds, petitioned the General Court for assistance, providing the only firsthand record of the encounter.

> The enemy...made a shot at your Petitioner and shot him through the wrist between the bones, and also made a large wound in his side. Which wounds have been very painful and costly to your Petitioner in the cure of them and have in a great measure utterly taken away the use of his left hand, and wholly taken him off from his employment this winter. Your Petitioner therefore humbly prays this honorable Court that they would make

him such compensation as shall seem fit, which he shall thankfully acknowledge, and doubts not but will be an encouragement to others speedily to relieve their neighbors when assaulted by so barbarous an enemy.[70]

The General Court granted him forty pounds, but no further payments or pension. The capture of John Brown's family was the only recorded Indian attack on Newbury soil in its history, but conflicts involving Newbury families in other parts of New England would continue well into the next century.

END OF THE CENTURY

The long and fruitful seventeenth century closed in Newbury with two parishes, a long drought and an amazing discovery in the woods. In 1697, James Noyes, nephew of the minister of the same name, came across some odd rock formations in the woods of Newbury, near the Little River. They were limestone, a precious commodity to the first settlers. Lime had been made in Newbury for decades from pulverizing oyster and clam shells, a tedious, labor-intensive process. Lime was used for chimneys, wall plastering and stone facing, and the town realized quickly that it needed control of this new resource or it would disappear.

Devil's Den, the colorful name later given to the limestone formations discovered in 1697. *From Currier's "Ould Newbury."*

William Dummer, Richard Dummer's grandson, who gave money for the founding of Governor Dummer Academy in 1763. *Private collection.*

The Governor Dummer mansion, built circa 1712. *Private collection.*

Sure enough, before long, thirty wagons a day were hauling limestone away without anyone's permission, and the town put together a committee, headed by the limestone's intrepid discoverer, to regulate its use and issue fines for theft. The town built a lime kiln not far from the meetinghouse for public use. In 1698, no more limestone was allowed to be sold out of the town, and the quarry was able to supply the community well into the nineteenth century.

The end of the century also saw the end of many of the town's prominent founders. Richard Dummer died in 1679 at the age of eighty-eight, and his friend and fellow church dissenter, John Emery, died in 1683, aged eighty-four. Both left sons of the same name in Newbury to carry on their businesses, and both families would leave significant marks on the history of the town. Governor Dummer Academy was founded in 1763 with a bequest from Richard Dummer's grandson, William, an acting governor of Massachusetts Bay, and descendants of John Emery gave money and land for the building of All Saints Church and Emery House retreat center in West Newbury. John Woodbridge, their fellow settler and old adversary, died in 1691.

CHAPTER 18

EXECUTION, 1701

*She was a poor sinful creature, as vile as ordinarily any are under the light of the gospel,
and one, who had a child by a negro at Newbury, when she was about seventeen years of
age, as she herself confessed, and that she murdered it and buried it in the garden, and
four years after had a child again and murdered that, but could not conceal it.*
—Fairfield's journal, July 15, 1701[71]

The eighteenth century began with a mild winter, a new meetinghouse and a grisly
murder. Its first half would see many prominent Newbury citizens leave their
Puritan brethren and return to the Church of England and the waterfront develop into
a thriving boomtown. As merchants, sailors and wharf rats plied their trades along the
port of Newbury, they would eventually see the need to separate from the rural "Old
Town," and the year 1764 would see the end of Old Newbury.

By 1700, however, there were still only two houses hard by the water near Watt's
Cellar, though there had been a flurry of applications over the preceding five years
to build docks, wharves and shipbuilding establishments. Ezra Cottle began building
ships at the bottom of Chandler's Lane (Federal Street), Stephen Greenleaf was given
permission to build a wharf and ships and tavern keeper Hugh March built a wharf near
his barn. Shipbuilding was also likely taking place on the narrow strip of town-owned
riverfront land, which was later divided up as river lots; men who used the building yard
there were charged "threepence per ton (of ship's weight)."

In the closing years of the seventeenth century, the members of the first parish in
Newbury decided they had outgrown their meetinghouse and began building a new one
nearby. Reverend John Richardson, who had brought a measure of religious peace to
the community following the turbulent latter tenure of Thomas Parker, died in 1696,
and Christopher Toppan, who had briefly ministered at the west parish church, agreed
to take over the original Newbury congregation (now known as the first parish, since the
west end was the second).

At the end of 1698, an agreement was made with Stephen Jaques to build a sixty- by
fifty-foot meetinghouse with twenty-four-foot ceilings. The new meetinghouse was to be
a thorough do-over, with a new pulpit and a new bell. It was a very impressive building,
with soaring ceilings and an upper gallery. A century later, Newbury minister John

OLD-TOWN MEETING-HOUSE, 1700–1806.

This meetinghouse was located across the street from the current First Parish Meeting House and served the parish for over one hundred years. It was replaced with a larger building in 1806. *Private collection.*

Popkin remembered it thus:

> *The roof was constructed with four gable ends, or projections, one on each side, each containing a large window, which gave light to the upper galleries. The turret was in the center. The space within was open to the roof, where was visible plenty of timber, with great needles and little needles pointing downwards, which served at once for strength and ornament. There were many ornaments of antique sculpture and wainscot. It was a stately building in the day of it.*[72]

The Spencer-Peirce-Little House, built by Colonel Daniel Peirce in 1690. *Courtesy of Reginald W. Bacon.*

The new meetinghouse was completed in the winter of 1699, and by October 1700, a committee was still deciding the tricky issue of pew seating. Daniel Peirce, who had led the search for the Brown family five years before, got the first choice of pew, a sign of very high status in the community. Peirce's wealth was substantial. In 1690, he had built a massive, old-style English manor house of stone and brick on what had been John Spencer's land. He had imported the brick and limestone, and unlike many of his neighbors, he built his house in the middle of his property, a sign of his baronial self-image. He spent a fortune on its construction, and it remains one of the architectural wonders of New England.

Once Daniel Peirce had picked out his meetinghouse pew, other local dignitaries (and contributors to the construction of the meetinghouse) were given permission to choose their seats. The committee assigned the rest. In all, 313 people had a seat in the meetinghouse by 1701, with more members born or moving into the community each year. Even this large, impressive meetinghouse was stuffed to the gills.

THE WAGES OF SIN

On July 31, 1701, twenty-one-year-old Esther (or Hester) Rogers climbed the scaffold in Ipswich and was hanged for infanticide before a crowd of over four thousand people. She was the first woman to hang in Ipswich in its history, and people came from miles around to see the spectacle. Before she died, she made a statement warning all the young people in the crowd to learn from her mistakes and avoid bad company and descent into sin.

Esther Rogers had first found bad company in Newbury, where she was apprenticed at age thirteen. It had started out well enough: she was taught to read and write and study the Bible, but when another servant in the household, a "Negro lad," caught her attention, she entered into a lively teenage affair. When a pregnancy resulted, however, a frightened Esther carried the baby to term undetected, smothered it at birth and buried it in her master's garden. She was seventeen. Two years later she completed her apprenticeship and went to work in a tavern out of town, but she was back within a year and once again became pregnant. For the second time, she carried the baby to term undetected, gave birth and, as tradition has it, drowned the newborn in the pond behind the meetinghouse.

This time, however, she was caught, arrested and imprisoned in Newbury in November 1700. At her trial in Boston, Newbury constable John Pike submitted a receipt for his expenses for "seizing and securing the body of Hester Rogers of said Newbury, apprehended by one of his majesty's justices for murdering her children in the year 1700."

Esther Rogers was transferred from Newbury to Ipswich jail, where she confessed her crimes and sought the company of several ministers. In Ipswich she experienced a prison conversion of such depth of feeling that, though it did not defer her execution, it profoundly affected all who tended to her. One minister, John Rogers (no apparent relation), wrote that she approached her death with such

> *composure of spirit, cheerfulness of countenance, pleasantness of speech, and a sort of complaisance in carriage towards the ministers who were assistant to her, [that she] melted the hearts of all that were within seeing or hearing, into tears of affection.*[73]

As it swung from its rope, Reverend Samuel Belcher of Newbury described Esther Rogers's body as "consecrated fruit," and he declared her "a pillar of salt transformed into a monument of free grace."

Later, in 1701, Belcher, John Rogers and the other ministers involved in the case collaborated on a cautionary book based on Esther Rogers's story, called *Death the Certain Wages of Sin to the Impenitent: Life the Sure Reward of Grace to the Penitent: Together with the Only Way for Youth to Avoid the Former, and Attain the Latter.*

It does not appear that Esther Rogers ever named her children's father, and there was not enough evidence to try anyone for fornication or accomplice to murder;

Rear view of the First Parish Church showing Meeting House Pond. *Courtesy of Historic New England.*

however, Joshua Coffin closes his account of the case by noting that three months after Rogers's execution, Thomas Mossum, "a colored man," was ordered out of Newbury with his family.

Byfield

Life went on as usual in Newbury during the months-long imprisonment and trial of Esther Rogers, though most of the town turned out to see her execution. The new meetinghouse was being built across the road from Tristram Coffin Jr.'s house, Richard Brown was settling in as the new schoolmaster and preaching sermons for Reverend Toppan when he fell ill and nineteen families in the southwest corner of Newbury and adjacent parts of Rowley were growing tired of traveling for miles to come to meeting.

Milestone 33 is dated 1708 and is located in Byfield, hence the mileage given to Newbury (five). *HABS photograph.*

BYFIELD CHURCH, NEWBURY, MASS.
Built, 1746. Burnt, 1833.

Byfield Parish Church. This is the second church built after the incorporation of Byfield Parish. *Courtesy of Historic New England.*

In 1701, these families successfully petitioned the town to relieve them of half their "minister's rate"; with those savings, they purchased land and erected a meetinghouse the following year. They hired Reverend Moses Hale to be their minister and built him a parsonage in 1703. Unlike the split with the west parish, this southern division seems to have gone off without a hitch, with both Rowley and Newbury congregations releasing their far-flung brethren from their tax obligations by 1704.

The residents of this new parish decided to call themselves "Byfield," after Colonel (later Judge) Nathaniel Byfield of Boston, apparently hoping this honor would produce a significant financial gift from its namesake. Colonel Byfield was rather more shocked than flattered and wrote to the town:

> *I am surprised at the account you give me of a new town upon the River Parker near Newbury. How they hit upon my name I can't imagine. I heartily wish them prosperity; and if any respect to me was the cause, it is an obligation upon me, (when God shall enable me) to study how I may be serviceable to them.*

When, several years later, Colonel Byfield had not ponied up, Judge Samuel Sewell, grandson of the Henry Sewell who had gone very publicly senile years before, took up the cause. In 1707, he wrote:

> *Sir, The enclosed news-letter mentions the little parish, that bears your name, and was so called for your sake. The parishioners have struggled with many difficulties in their little and low beginnings. The work they have accomplished is noble. They have settled the worship of God in a place where the inhabitants were under very hard circumstances, by reason of their remoteness. Their hands are few, and weak. If you shall find in your heart, one way or other to give them a lift, I am persuaded, you will therein be a worker with God.*[74]

It was another three years before Colonel Byfield gave to the new parish. In 1710, he presented a bell weighing 226 pounds to celebrate the congregation's independent status, approved a few weeks earlier by the General Court.

CHAPTER 19

NEWBURY MILITIAMEN
IN THE FIELD, 1700–1710

*Colonel John March was a tyro set over a crowd of ploughboys, fishermen, and mechanics, officered
by tradesmen, farmers, blacksmiths, village magnates, and deacons of the church—for the characters
of deacon and militia officer were often joined in one. These improvised soldiers commonly did well in
small numbers, and very ill in large ones.*
—Frances Parkman, A Half-Century of Conflict (1892)[75]

When Colonel Nathaniel Byfield was but a captain, in 1697, he was sent to York,
Maine, to the aid of Major John March of Newbury. John March spent the next
decade fighting Indians allied with the French up and down the coast of Maine, and he
was in command of the Casco Bay (Portland) fort in 1702, when, after a brief peace,
France again declared war on England and therefore the colony. This conflict is known
to history as Queen Anne's War (1702–1713).

On August 18, 1703, Major March and thirty-six men were guarding the Casco
garrison when it was approached by a small group of previously friendly chiefs.
According to Francis Parkman's *A Half-Century of Conflict*, John March went out to meet
them with two older men.

> *They had hardly reached the spot when the three chiefs drew hatchets…and sprang upon
> them, while other Indians, ambushed near by, leaped up and joined in the attack. The two
> old men were killed at once; but March, who was noted for strength and agility, wrenched
> a hatchet from one of his assailants, and kept them all at bay.*[76]

Other soldiers finally arrived and drove the natives off, but they soon reappeared,
burning and looting the cabins on the outskirts of the garrison, forcing all of the
townspeople inside. Soon, John March and his thirty-six soldiers were defending the
fort against some five hundred men, who spent three days digging into the ramparts
surrounding the garrison before they were frightened off by an incoming ship.

Two months later, John March petitioned the General Court to help him recoup some
of his losses. He had left

his own habitation in Newbury and removed his family stock of cattle and other estate to the said fort, by which means, upon the perfidious breach lately made by that barbarous people, your petitioner was in utmost hazard of losing his life.

His losses included "eight oxen, fourteen cows, ten calves, thirty-six swine, twenty-five sheep, five acres of wheat, six acres of peas, fifty bushels of oats, and various articles of furniture and clothing."[77] For his trouble, John March was granted fifty pounds and promoted to lieutenant colonel. He also decided to sell his family's ferry in Newbury to the town.

It was not the last time March would see action against the French and their native allies, however. In December 1703, the General Court laid a special forty-pound bounty on the scalps of Indians above ten years of age, and in an attempt to pursue and destroy the natives in their winter encampments, the Court also instructed military companies to outfit their men with snowshoes and moccasins for a winter campaign. John March found forty men from Hampton and twenty-eight from Newbury willing to serve as "snowshoe men."

Though they were trained and outfitted for winter fighting, the men spent the summer of 1704 employed instead at building and guarding blockhouses from Newbury to Bradford. Blockhouses were generally solid log structures with a second story overhanging the first. Gun ports in the upper story enabled its defenders to shoot down at the enemy, sometimes with cannon, and slits in the walls of the first floor allowed for firing straight on. Over the season, thirty-two Newbury men submitted bills for their service at the blockhouses, but by winter, additional deployments for a major campaign were underway.

In January 1705, two companies of soldiers, some from Newbury, marched through snow four feet deep to Norridgewock, Maine, north of Augusta. It was a brutal march, 165 miles in the dead of winter, and when the group arrived, the Indians had been warned and fled, along with a Jesuit priest, leaving their fort unprotected. The soldiers burned the fort and a small church with it.

While marching home empty-handed, Nathaniel Rolfe of Newbury, nephew of the flirtatious Mary Rolfe, was shot in the arm, and upon his return, he asked the General Court to compensate him for his pain. Apparently it was a nasty wound, requiring

visits, balsams, injections, plasters, urgents, and dressing his arm…following to the perfecting of the cure of a large gun shot wound in his arm with a laceration of nerves and follicles, [and for] *specifics and medicines proper for him in an acute and dangerous fever which ran fourteen days.*

Nathaniel Rolfe was granted twenty pounds and was temporarily relieved of duty.

Another trek to Norridgewock was attempted the following year, but it was abandoned when mild winter weather turned the tracks to mud and made rivers impassable. In March 1707, John March was sent out again, this time with seventy or eighty men, to sail from Newbury to the Kennebec River, where they fought a group of Indians and returned home. Meanwhile, the General Court had resolved that the only way to halt the attacks on its northern frontier was to invade French Canada, and John March was given the honor of being appointed commander in chief of an attack on Port Royal, Nova Scotia.

Over a thousand men in sixty-eight vessels were put under March's command, including two Newbury companies. On May 13, they set sail from Nantasket, on Cape Cod, and arrived at Port Royal thirteen days later. From the beginning, the expedition was a disaster. The fort was well defended, and French troops drove March's men into the woods, where they were easily ambushed. An effort to destroy French ships in the harbor was abandoned when a rumor began that they were booby-trapped.

After five days and over a hundred casualties, March called off the attack and, with his men, sailed for Casco Bay to await further orders. John March was tired and disheartened, and when operations in Nova Scotia were put under the direction of an officers' commission, he wrote to the Massachusetts governor, clearly wishing to be relieved of duty:

> [I] *have not been justly dealt with by those who have informed your Excellency, but since it is your Excellency's pleasure to dismiss me from those commands you were formerly pleased to put in me, I will patiently bear it, and do you what service lies in my power. Since it is so, I would have been glad if you would have been pleased to have released me, for I certainly know that if there be anything well and honorably done, I shall have no share in that, but if anything fall out otherwise, that will fall to my share.*[78]

When his ships landed at Port Royal once again on August 10, he could not even bring himself to leave his ship, and he turned over command of the expedition to his subordinate officer. Fourteen days later, they sailed home, defeated once again.

John March was booed and hissed in Boston. Children ran after him, calling out "wooden sword," and he was nearly the subject of a court-martial. Later commentators, however, have placed the blame for such military failures on the colonial leadership more broadly, for the colonists were stubbornly independent and refused to give over command of their missions to professional British officers. March has been described as a rather pathetic figure, "a tyro set over a crowd of ploughboys, fishermen, and mechanics."[79] John March apparently retired to Woodbridge, New Jersey, after this humiliation, and Port Royal was finally taken in 1710.

While John March was struggling to defend the northern borders of the colony, the ragtag militiamen left in Newbury were called upon to defend the Merrimack to the west. Thomas Noyes, commander of the Newbury regiment in 1705, sent a contingent of twenty men to defend Haverhill; the Haverhill commander was unimpressed with the selection, however, and wrote Noyes a scathing note:

> *I received your return of the twenty men the Governor commanded me to call for, and when the persons (which I can't call men) appeared…a considerable number of them* [were] *but boys, or children, and not fit for service, blind in part, and deaf, and cross-handed.*

One was so unfit that he was sent back, with a request that Noyes "send some able man in his place, if you have an able one in Newbury."[80] Another group of Newbury men was sent to guard the far shore of the Merrimac River between Amesbury and Haverhill.

In 1707, twenty-one-year-old Samuel Bartlett was drafted from Newbury into service in Haverhill. In August 1708, he was sleeping at the house of Captain Wainwright when the town was attacked. The house was quickly surrounded, Wainwright was killed and the other members of the house surrendered and were carried away. Samuel Bartlett was taken all the way to Montreal, where he lived first with the Indians and then as a servant to a French merchant. He was ransomed in 1712 and came home to Newbury after four years, two months and nine days. The General Court paid him twenty pounds. In the same attack on Haverhill, a minister, Benjamin Rolfe, was killed, along with his wife and child. He was the brother of Nathaniel Rolfe, who was shot on the road heading back from Norridgewock, Maine.

Difficult as it is to imagine how life could go on as normal when all available men were either in Haverhill or Amesbury or guarding the blockhouses, everyday life in Newbury continued. However, yet another perennial threat to communal peace and harmony loomed on the horizon. Another battle over a meetinghouse was about to begin, and this one would change the town forever.

CHAPTER 20

DISSENTING DISSENTERS

Anglican Again

Twenty-two in all, declaring that they were of the pure episcopal church of England, would no longer persist with their mistaken dissenting brethren, had sent to their diocesan, the bishop of London for a minister and desired protection.
—*Diary of Samuel Sewall, February 27, 1712*

When the second, western parish in Newbury was established in 1695, the meetinghouse had been built on "the Plains," at the west end of what is now Newburyport. However, a majority of the new congregation had always felt that the meetinghouse would be better situated at Pipestave Hill, three miles farther down the Bradford Road. In 1706, when growth made a new meetinghouse necessary, the town sided with the majority of the west parish, voting to move the meetinghouse to Pipestave Hill. It was further agreed that construction on the new building would begin, but the taxes to pay for it would not start coming due until 1709.

This move was vehemently contested by the minority of the congregation, who wished to remain in the Plains meetinghouse, and in 1709, when the tax levy came into effect, fifty-five petitioners wrote to the General Court begging that, if no other resolution were possible, they be allowed to form yet another, third parish, "to maintain our minister and ministry amongst ourselves, the [cost] whereof we choose abundantly to undergo rather than have our good ends, desires and endeavors… frustrated and made void."[81]

Thomas Noyes wrote to the General Court on behalf of the town, noting with evident irritation that most of the petitioners had had no part in paying for construction of the Plains meetinghouse, that some of them lived closer to Pipestave Hill anyway and that several of them actually lived within a mile of the first parish meetinghouse. The sense of building a new meetinghouse farther to the west was clear, "yet rather than not have their wills they would have two churches." The Plains families retorted that if it meant the spiritual care and nurture of their families, then yes, they wanted two churches.

In 1710, the General Court sided with the town, sending a strongly worded letter to the Plains families informing them that the official meetinghouse of the west parish would be at Pipestave Hill and that a tax would be charged to the entire parish for the completion of the new meetinghouse. Twenty-seven congregants signed a letter pledging to continue to support a minister at the old meetinghouse on the Plains, despite being "forced to pay elsewhere what shall be levied upon us."[82]

In the spring of 1711, the west parish voted to appoint a committee

> *to take the seats and boards and glass out of the old meeting house, to be improved in the new meeting house, and also to remove the old meeting house and set it up at Pipe-stave hill to be improved for a barn for the ministry.*

Not only were the Plains families losing their meetinghouse, but they were also to suffer the indignity of having it turned into a barn.

The parish, with its formal vote and appointed committee, backed up by the will of the General Court, appeared committed to acting according to the letter of the law in the removal of the Plains meetinghouse. In the event, however, the demolition seems to have gone forward in a less than professional manner. Perhaps anticipating physical resistance from the Plains congregants, a group of men from the Pipestave congregation, according to Joshua Coffin, "came down in a riotous and disorderly manner, in the night, tore down the old meeting house, and carried it off."[83] When the neighbors woke the next morning, the building that had been their center of worship for over fifteen years was gone.

The Plains families were more determined than ever to have their own meetinghouse. The General Court soon received a petition from the town, saying that the rebellious faction was furiously cutting and hauling timber and "intend to raise said meetinghouse within one fortnight and set it at or near the east end of the west precinct in Newbury as they inform us, not regarding the late resolve of the great and General Court." The new Plains meetinghouse was going up near the site of the one that had just been pulled down. All hope of reconciliation in the west parish was gone, and when the General Court intervened and ordered the Plains congregants to stop work on the building until the Court could reconvene, they refused.

The town was in a panic by August, and again petitioned the General Court, complaining that the rebels had "raised and in part covered a meeting house." This time the Court came down more harshly and ordered that the workers be "served by the sheriff with a process and order of this Court...strictly forbidding them and their associates proceeding in the work of their intended meeting house." They were also summoned to court, where, on November 2, 1711, a final verdict was rendered. Unlike the previous separations, which resulted in Byfield and the west end becoming separate parishes, this one came down on the side of the established congregation:

> *Upon hearing the case of Newbury referring to the house late pretended to be raised for the public worship of God on or near deacon Joshua Brown's land, contrary to the direction of this Court, of which there is no present necessity: It is ordered that the building of the said house be not on any pretence whatever further proceeded in but that the division of the town into two precincts between the old meeting house and that upon Pipe-stave hill be the present division of the [town] and is hereby confirmed and established and all persons concerned are to yield obedience accordingly, and that the disorders, that have been*

in the proceedings about the said house in Brown's land, be referred to the next sessions of peace in Essex.[84]

In other words, the new meetinghouse—to which the General Court would only deign to refer as a "house"—was to be abandoned, and the matter referred to the county court. The Plains men were in a difficult situation. No matter how strongly they felt about their right to separate, they would not be able to hire a new minister under such a strict order from the General Court; fines and even imprisonment could follow for the minister and his congregation under such circumstances. On the other hand, the Plains congregants were still aggrieved and outraged at the Court, the town and the Pipestave congregation, and they resolved not to keep company with the men who had so violently torn down their church. There was only one power greater than the General Court and the governor to whom they could appeal: they went straight to the queen of England, through a minor official named John Bridger.

John Bridger was not a popular man in the colony. His position as "surveyor of the king's (or queen's) woods" meant that he was able to claim that most valuable commodity—timber—in the name of the Crown. It was John Bridger who marked trees with the queen's arrow for the use of the English navy, and he could turn in his neighbors if their floorboards were too wide (meaning they had cut down trees large enough to be used as masts). He was also a devout Anglican, a member of the very Church of England the Puritans saw as corrupt and had come to America to escape. To the Plains congregation of Newbury, however, Bridger offered a way to escape the tyranny of their Puritan brethren, by returning to the parent church.

When the families, outraged by the destruction of their meetinghouse, called on John Bridger to help them come under the protection of the Church of England, in the eyes of their neighbors they were committing a grave sin at best and treason at worst. Nonetheless, on February 27, 1712, Joseph Bailey of the renegade Newbury congregation went to the governor with Bridger and two other Anglicans to present a declaration of their intention to leave the church. Signed by twenty-two petitioners, it affirmed that "they were of the pure episcopal church of England" and had sent to London for a minister.[85]

The governor, Joseph Dudley, was himself part of a small Anglican community in Boston, but he was charged with keeping the colony in good order, and the schism in Newbury would be extraordinarily controversial. Still, he could not very well object to their request, particularly since they had already asked the Bishop of London for an Anglican minister. The Newbury men were also in fear for their safety and needed assurance from the governor that they "may not be molested in the future upon this account." On February 28, Governor Dudley granted their petition to separate:

I am thereupon of opinion that the said petitioners and others that join with them ought to be peaceably allowed in their lawful proceedings therein for their good establishment; and ought not to be taxed or imposed upon for the support and maintenance of any other public worship in the said town.[86]

St. Anna's Chapel, next to Saint Paul's Episcopal Church, was named after Anna Maria, daughter of Reverend Horton, who died of tuberculosis in 1857. Photograph by George E. Noyes. *Courtesy of Historic New England.*

This was one of the most scandalous developments in the town to that date. Whatever its internal quarrels, Newbury had always been Puritan in its views. In 1635, Thomas Millward of Newbury had been imprisoned for an act of protest against the established English church: He cut the cross out of the flag flown over a Boston fort. A prominent Newbury resident, Judge Samuel Sewell, had refused to serve in a military company whose sign was a cross. Now, some of the same Newbury men whose fathers had fought Reverend Thomas Parker tooth and nail to preserve the congregational form of church governance—which utterly rejected the hierarchy of the Anglican establishment—were now joining the Church of England.

Not everyone believed that this split was due to a true change in religious belief. Reverend Benjamin Coleman of Boston wrote to Bishop White Kennet of Peterborough, England, that the newly Anglican Newbury congregation was

> *utterly ignorant of the church they declare for, nor offended in the least with the form of worship or discipline which they turn from…* [They] *would before this have disowned me in particular for the use of the Lord's Prayer, reading the scriptures and a freer admission to the Lord's table.*[87]

Regardless of their motivations, the Plains congregation in Newbury was readily accepted by the Church of England. Within a few months of their petition to the governor, an English organization known as the Society for the Propagation of the Gospel in Foreign Parts, founded in 1701 to encourage the spread of the Anglican Church throughout the world, sent a naval chaplain to tend to the small flock at the Plains. Reverend John Lambton arrived in Newbury to find that his determined congregation had built and furnished a substantial building for him to preach in, with over two hundred people gathered to welcome him. The church was named Queen Anne's Chapel, after the ruling monarch, and was located along the road to Bradford, now Storey Avenue in Newburyport.

Reverend Lambton headed a congregation that was both proud of its opposition to the rest of the town and also afraid of the consequences of its decision. With a church, a minister and permission from the governor to assemble, it seemed that the congregation's position was unassailable; however, the town did not release it so easily. Several men were thrown in jail on the pretext that they had not paid their taxes. One by one, the heads of the new Anglican families were called upon to explain their absence from the meetinghouse and were fined.

In March 1713, even though the Anglican minister had been in place for at least six months, eight Plains men were brought before a parish committee and questioned. They responded with three distinct reasons for their separation:

> *First, we do count that you acted illegally in disposing of a house that you never built. Second, for violently pulling down our meeting house and carrying it away contrary to our minds and consent. Third, taking away from our brethren and neighbors part of their estates by distress.*

None of them mentioned any quarrels with the doctrine or beliefs of the old church.

Map of the west parish of Newbury in 1729. Queen Anne's Chapel is number 13, and the Pipestave Meeting House is number 56. *From Currier's* "Ould Newbury."

The following year, the west parish, now settled in at its new meetinghouse on Pipestave Hill, finally voted to release its neighbors from parish obligations and taxes. The long struggle in the west parish was over, at least for the time being. But now the Plains congregation was faced with another problem. Converting to Anglicanism had been a powerful weapon in their struggle for independence, but many of the newly minted Newbury Anglicans were unfamiliar and uncomfortable with the traditions of their new church. After an anxious series of meetings, Reverend Lambton agreed to forgo some of the more controversial aspects of the service.

Reverend Christopher Toppan, of the first parish church, wrote to Cotton Mather in Boston:

> *Perceiving that some of the ceremonies were camels too big for them at first to swallow,* [Rev. Lambton] *told them they should be left to their liberty as to kneeling at the sacrament, baptizing with the sign of the cross and so forth. This has been wonderfully taking with them and a great means to encourage them in their factious proceedings.*

St. Paul's Episcopal Church. This building was destroyed by fire in 1920 and was replaced with a stone building. *Courtesy of the Newburyport Public Library.*

Toppan blamed the colonial government for not having "the courage to stand by their own established laws"; instead, he suggested, "through a spirit of cowardice, they shrink in their shoulders and are afraid to appear for Christ and the interest of religion among us."[88]

In any case, for the moment, whatever personal harassment the new congregation in Newbury faced, it was at least safe from further court proceedings. It was also not afraid to ask for help from the Society and was given money to supplement the funds it had raised for Lambton's salary and the valuable books and sacramental articles necessary for Anglican worship.

The determined little congregation at Queen Anne's Chapel thus got off to a rocky, but ultimately successful, start. However, in 1720 it suffered an extraordinary tragedy. The first minister, John Lambton, had resigned due to poor health in 1714, and Reverend Henry Lucas had been transferred from Braintree to replace him. There was a bit of bad feeling in the church when Reverend Lucas arrived. The congregation had been without a minister for nearly a year, and some of the members had begun to meet in private homes, taking some of the books and communion silver with them. Though Henry Lucas seems to have brought the congregation back together, he was never able to win their full support and sympathy. Suffering from deep depression and disillusionment, he committed suicide in 1720 by cutting his own throat. The stunned congregation allowed a full funeral and church burial, honors not often afforded suicide victims.

The church was temporarily tended by the occasional services of the nearest Anglican minister, Reverend David Mossum of Marblehead, until the arrival of Reverend Matthias Plant in 1722. The congregation at Queen Anne's Chapel prospered under Reverend Plant, and in 1740 he would oversee the erection of a second house of worship, St. Paul's Church, at the head of Market Street, which eventually replaced the Plains meetinghouse and grew into the vibrant Episcopal congregation that still worships there today.

CHAPTER 21

EXPANSION AND
THE GREAT AWAKENING

The Lord is pleased to make quick work of it. Some convinced, humbled to the dust and converted in
a minute, others in an hour—others in a night and others longer—to see them under convictions and
in such an extraordinary concern, so that the most acute or most sharp pain of body that ever I saw
is [not in] any way comparable to it—and how should it be, since Solomon tells us that the spirit of
a man sustaineth his infirmity, but a wounded spirit, who can bear—they are indeed pricked in their
heart and cry out what shall we do.
—Letter from Edmund Coffin to his father, October 14, 1741[89]

The life of church and school were intertwined in colonial New England. Ministers often taught school before being appointed to churches, and they often tutored older students in Latin and Greek. In the seventeenth century, the Reverends Thomas Parker and John Woodbridge had both spent time teaching the first generations of Newbury boys (girls were taught at home). Newbury consistently had a difficult time recruiting and maintaining a schoolmaster, particularly since education was neither free nor compulsory. Fees were paid out of a combination of town and private money, with parents often unable to afford to send their children to school or to spare them in the fields.

Schoolmasters in Newbury were a particularly unhappy lot. In 1680, a Mr. Emerson took the town to court for illegally dismissing him after he asked for a raise. When Richard Brown was hired in 1699, he was expected not only to keep the grammar school, but also to preach once a month and substitute for the ministers of the first and second parish. His pay was only half as much as a minister's. He was also the town clerk. In October 1701, he took a position in Reading, where he would later serve as a minister, and on his way out of Newbury he left a nasty note in the town's birth and death register:

I have served Newbury as schoolmaster eleven years and an half and as town clerk about
five years and have been repaid with abuse, contempt and ingratitude…Those I have bred
think themselves better than their master…I pray that poor unacknowledging Newbury
may get them that may serve them better and find thanks when they have done. If to find
a house for the school two years, when the town had none, gratis, if to take the scholars

J. CURRIER J?., SHIP YARD.

BELLEVILLE

The west end of Newburyport, known as Belleville, was home to several shipyards and was briefly its own town in the eighteenth century. *Courtesy of Susan Follansbee.*

View of Newburyport harbor in the late nineteenth century. *Courtesy of Susan Follansbee.*

to my own fire when there was no wood at school as frequently, if to give records to the poor, and record their births and deaths gratis deserves acknowledgements, then it is my due, but hard to come by.[90]

By 1717, the town was so large that it voted to divide itself administratively into four districts and hire four schoolmasters, who also were expected to divide their school year among multiple neighborhoods. Their lessons were based on the Bible and the *New England Primer*, published in 1695, supplemented by a lengthy catechism written by James Noyes and memorized by every Newbury child. The town contributed not only to the building of Harvard College, but also to its student body, with over three hundred Newbury men graduating between 1642 and 1840.

The waterfront was also growing in leaps and bounds in the first decades of the eighteenth century, and Newbury was rapidly becoming a real port town. Not only were wharves and ferries appearing all along the Merrimack River, but there were also significant shipbuilding operations. Between 1697 and 1714, one hundred vessels were registered in Newbury and allowed to join the coastal trade. There were shipyards at the bottom of Federal Street, Market Street, Marlboro Street, near Thurlow's Bridge over the Parker River, on Carr's Island and near Watt's Cellar.

There was growing concern about the amount of liquor available to men in the port, and in 1718, the town voted to have no more than five taverns serving beer and wine and three retailers of hard liquor. Fifty years before, the town had subsidized the taverns and asked Paul White to sell his spirits to the town for religious and medicinal purposes, but those days were gone.

A new rule that all roads had to be four rods wide spurred a flurry of road building and repair, and a ferry to Haverhill was established in the west parish, the present site of the Rocks Village Bridge. Newbury's port was becoming more and more distinct from the rural Old Town, where Newbury began, and the west parish, best known for its sprawling farms and sheep.

By 1722, the population near the water had grown so large that the residents there petitioned for, and were granted, permission to form a new parish, the third in Newbury. If there was any real dispute over this separation, it is absent from the record. The first parish gave its permission without recorded argument on September 17. The new meetinghouse was built in the heart of the bustling waterfront, in the center of what is known today as Market Square. By 1726, the residents had signed their church covenant, hired a minister and fixed the boundaries of their new parish.

Considering the agony that had attended the birth of the second parish—not to mention the establishment of the Anglican church on the Plains—the third went off without a hitch. It is likely that since so many wealthy and influential members of the first parish left to join the third, there was not much will to fight their departure. A decade after the split, the meetinghouse was enlarged to a massive eighty by sixty feet, with two galleries. The first parish congregation voted to donate its old bell, which the third parish accepted. The first, second and third parish churches also decided to come together in a new way. In 1727, representatives from each parish formed the

Cattle pens by Frog Pond. This area, now a park, was used as common pasture after the center of town moved in 1646. *Courtesy of the Historical Society of Old Newbury.*

first council of churches, "to meet once a month and consider what may be for the good of the town in general, especially the churches in it and more particularly their own church."[91]

Since the bustling port cared for the dead as well as the living, a new burying ground was laid out near Frog Pond (now Old Hill Burying Ground, above Bartlett Mall), and the following year it was enclosed with a board fence. The new third parish also voted "to set their school house by frog pond," and to build a courthouse on Federal Street. The courthouse was built in 1735 at the top of Marlboro Street, a compromise with the first parish, but still convenient to the port. In 1741, a fourth parish was divided off from the Pipestave congregation, comprising the extreme westerly end of Newbury by the Bradford border.

Disease, Earthquakes and a Strange Beast

On April 19, 1723, Daniel Holbrook, the assistant minister in the first parish, was delivering a funeral sermon when he suddenly became ill and was forced to leave the pulpit. He was dead the next day. Throughout April, wave after wave of diphtheria spread through Newbury, and at the end of the month, nearly forty people were dead, "most of them grown up, sometimes two a day, sometimes three a day, young men and women"[92] Periodic epidemics swept though Newbury, as happened in all towns. Port towns were particularly vulnerable, however, as new diseases arrived with the ships and carried off adults, as well as children.

In 1721, a terrible smallpox epidemic hit Boston, killing over eight hundred people. The town of Newbury was spared, and it sent loads of wood into the city to help residents get through the winter. The worst case of diphtheria in Newbury history began by the water in 1735 and continued for two years. The toll was awful:

> *A sickness began by the water side about September at Thomas Smith's, which carried off two of his children and prevailed among the children, so that by the middle of February there died from Chandler's lane* [Federal Street] *with the falls eighty-one persons. John Boynton lost eight children. Benjamin Knight had three buried in one grave.*[93]

Stephen Jaques's wife had a premonition during these dark times—she saw a child's hand under the bed, but no child in the room. Within a week, three of her grandsons were dead. In 1736, thirteen Byfield families lost every one of their children.

To add to the general sense of doom, a flurry of earthquake activity began in the 1720s and continued until the 1760s. Reverend Matthias Plant of Queen Anne's Chapel described the quake of 1727 in great detail:

> *Being the Lord's day at forty minutes past ten the same evening, there was a most terrible, sudden, and amazing earthquake, which did damage to the greatest part of the neighborhood, shook and threw down tops of chimneys and in many places the earth opened a foot or more. It continued very terrible by frequently bursting and shocking our houses and lasted all that week…sometimes breaking with loud claps six times or oftener in a day.*[94]

In 1724, the first parish's Reverend Christopher Toppan sent a letter to Boston theologian Cotton Mather, who was deeply interested in the supernatural, describing another unsettling discovery. Three teenage boys had been chased by a two-headed snake, or amphisbaena, a powerful figure in classical mythology. After spending some time poking at it with a stick, the boys had killed the snake, and it had been subsequently examined by respected members of the community who testified that it was, indeed, a two-headed snake. There was some confusion, however, about whether the second head was on its tail or if the two heads were side by side at one end, which would be possible, as snakes are occasionally born conjoined. The whole episode was quite unsettling to the community and must have felt like another message, like the earthquake activity, about how far their congregation had gone astray.

A century later, John Greenleaf Whittier wrote a poem about the episode called "The Double-Headed Snake of Newbury." He did not believe the story and thought it had been cooked up by Cotton Mather and Reverend Toppan to keep the townspeople aware of God's displeasure.

A snake with two heads, lurking so near!—
Judge of the wonder, guess at the fear!
Think what ancient gossips might say,
Shaking their heads in their dreary way,
Between the meetings on Sabbath-day!
Cotton Mather came galloping down
All the way to Newbury town,
With his eyes agog and his ears set wide,
And his marvelous inkhorn at his side.

THE PLAINS CONGREGATION

By 1738, Queen Anne's Chapel on the Plains was no longer a center of suspicion and controversy; in fact, it counted some of the most prominent citizens of the port among its members. Men involved in trade were able to benefit from a close spiritual relationship with the mother country, and in 1725, visiting English captains and crews had been given a special pew in the chapel. In addition to the increasing wealth of its members, the congregation had been given a boost in 1735, when the colony had allowed it to receive the taxes paid by its members in "certificates," or proof that they attended the Anglican church and no other.

In 1738, the church voted, and Reverend Matthias Plant agreed, that the church should expand closer to the port for the convenience of its members, whose business and personal interests were increasingly clustered around the waterside. A piece of land was laid out at the top of Market Street, and in 1742, Reverend Plant was officially invited to preach at the new St. Paul's Church. There was still a vibrant congregation at Queen Anne's Chapel, however, and for nearly a decade, Reverend Plant tried to balance the interests of both congregations while they clamored for increased independence. The two churches functioned simultaneously for nearly twenty years, until the powerful families of the waterside congregation finally gained predominance. Services at Queen Anne's Chapel were slowly reduced, finally sputtering out completely in 1766.

The Plains area was once again in need of a viable church, and in 1761, several Plains families met at Queen Anne's to discuss a return to the congregational church.

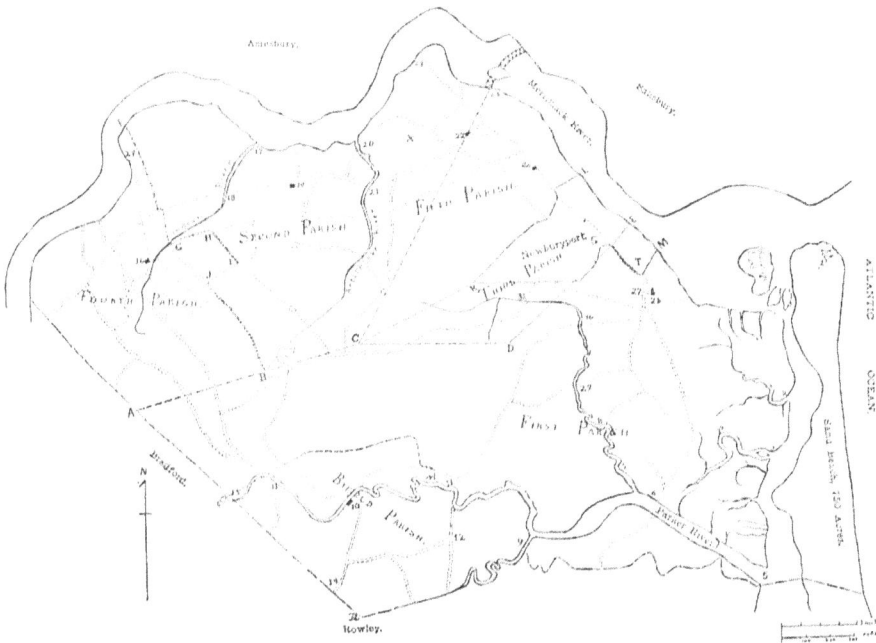

MAP OF NEWBURY — 1795.
SHOWING PARISH LINES.

Parish divisions in Newbury by 1795. *Currier's History of Newbury.*

After some heated exchanges with the new minister of St. Paul's, Reverend Edward Bass, the group was given permission to meet in the chapel while they built their own meetinghouse. In 1762, they gathered a congregation, hired a minister, split off as a fifth parish and completed construction of their own meetinghouse, leaving Queen Anne's Chapel derelict and abandoned. The building collapsed in 1770. Fifty years after the Plains men had left the Puritan church to the great distress and outrage of their neighbors, their children returned to the church for much the same reason: they didn't want to have to walk too far to meeting.

There is no doubt that most residents of Newbury had deep religious feeling, meetinghouse squabbles aside. In the few surviving personal documents that remain from that time, men and women search their souls at length for evidence of sin and examine their lives for signs of God's favor. All sorts of natural occurrences, from disease to floods to earthquakes, were earnestly examined as potential messages about where the community had displeased God. It is also clear, however, that as much as religion was a part of everyday life, for many it was primarily a social and community framework, providing hierarchy and structure based on who sat where in the meetinghouse, where the building was located, who had the best-educated minister, whose children were attending Harvard to become ministers themselves and so forth. The mental tallies kept at all social gatherings, from what your neighbors were wearing to whose servants were giggling during the service, became the stuff of many conversations in and about the church, while broader theological discussions were reserved for the minister and a few educated men.

Whatever the personal convictions of the men and women of Newbury in the 1730s and '40s, when the religious revival of the First Great Awakening swept through England and made its way to the colonies, they were ready to hear its fiery preachers and, in one memorable instance, to give the meetinghouse over to them.

Newbury's Great Awakening

George Whitefield was a fiery English preacher whose thundering sermons drew tens of thousands of people to great open-air revivals. Benjamin Franklin once calculated the volume of Whitfield's voice and determined that he could be heard by thirty thousand people. Whitefield preached an emotional and personal relationship with God, telling his listeners to come and repent of their sins. He ended his sermons with a call to action, urging them to return home and study the Bible, to leave their ministers if they were not satisfying their spiritual needs and, above all, to throw themselves at the mercy of God. Crowds went wild; men and women sobbed, swooned and knelt on the ground and howled.

Newbury's Edmund Coffin wrote to his father in 1741 describing an open-air meeting led by Whitefield's famous contemporary, Jonathan Edwards. Some of the attendees, he said, "humbled to the dust and converted in a minute, others in an hour—others in a night and others longer," in spiritual paroxysms exceeding in force those of "the most acute or most sharp pain of body that ever I saw." Primed for the experience, he said, "They admit of no meat, drink or sleep till they find rest for their souls in Christ."[95]

Whitefield and the other leaders of the Great Awakening quickly became the most famous men in America—the rock stars of the eighteenth century, one might say. In September 1740, Whitefield made his way to Newbury and preached there at the third parish meetinghouse in Market Square for the first time. He returned to Newbury some nine times over the course of his industrious travels, and his effect on the town was profound. In 1742, evangelical preachers known as "New Lights" successfully occupied the Market Square meetinghouse and preached there without permission to a riotous crowd.

They also attempted to take over the first parish meetinghouse, but since Cotton Mather's old friend Christopher Toppan was there, they were turned away. Matthias Plant, the minister at St. Paul's Church, wrote to a friend that he feared his church would be empty within six months, as "all the country near me is taken with this new scheme."

Two years after Whitefield's first meeting in Newbury, a small group of his dedicated followers built a small meetinghouse on High Street, near the top of Federal Street,

First Presbyterian meetinghouse on Federal Street, built in 1756. George Whitefield died in the house directly behind it. *Courtesy of the Historical Society of Old Newbury.*

and withdrew from their congregations. Christopher Toppan, minister of the first parish, lost nearly one hundred parishioners. He was outraged and wrote to one of the defectors, Charles Peirce, son of Colonel Daniel Peirce, calling him and the New Light preachers "schemers" and followers of Satan. By 1746, the new congregation hired a minister, Jonathan Parsons, who was among the most radical of the New Light preachers in New England.

Unlike the Anglican congregation of St. Paul's and local Quaker and Baptist congregations, whose members' church taxes could be used for their support, this new church, which became officially Presbyterian in 1748, was not recognized by the General Court. The Court refused to allow tax money to go to the new church. Until 1796, Newbury families who attended the new meetinghouse continued to be taxed by the first parish, despite decades of legal wrangling and petitions.

In 1756, the present Old South Church was built on Federal Street, and it was to this new meetinghouse, with its soaring steeple, square pews and oak frame, that George Whitefield came for the last time in 1770. He fell ill in the parsonage of the Old South Church, and Currier describes his last evening in detail:

> *Friends and neighbors had assembled in front of the parsonage, and even crowded into the hall to hear and see the wonderful preacher. He paused on the staircase, and began to speak to them. Although breathing with difficulty, he continued to exhort them "until the candle which he held in his hand burned away and went out in its socket.*"[96]

He died at six o'clock the next morning, September 30, and was buried, as he had requested, under the pulpit of the church that he had so inspired. In a demonstration of respect for a preacher whose views were so often at odds with their own, ministers from surrounding meetinghouses, including the first parish and St. Paul's, carried his coffin.

CHAPTER 22

MOSES TITCOMB AT LOUISBURG, 1745

*We are to Sail at two of ye Clock to morrow morning, and Pray God to Send us a good pasage theire
& Cover My hed in ye Day of Batel, and give me Suck Ses over my Enemys, which is, I trust, your
prayer for me. Remember my Cind Love to my wife & children & all other Frends.*
—Letter from Moses Titcomb to his brother, April 23, 1745

While Newbury residents searched their souls and established new congregations—including a Quaker meetinghouse in the fifth parish, the "Belleville" part of Newbury—and fought with great vigor over seemingly insignificant religious matters (a number of second parish families refused to attend church because their minister wore a wig and said that, unless he repented of that sin, he was "certainly damned"), they also looked with increasing anxiety northward, toward the French. These old colonial adversaries were amassing hostile settlements along the coast of southern Canada and around the St. Lawrence River.

In 1745, fishing and merchant vessels from Marblehead, Newbury, Salem and Boston were harassed and plundered by French privateers based in Louisburg, Nova Scotia. In response, an expedition was organized to attack and cripple the military installations there. Moses Titcomb, a thirty-eight-year-old officer from Newbury, was commissioned "major and captain of the third company in the Fifth Massachusetts Regiment," composed of fifty Newbury men, with one additional soldier from Haverhill and one from Beverly.

The company arrived in Nova Scotia on April 23 and was quickly involved in lugging cannons and supplies to batteries from which it pounded the fort and town of Louisburg for forty-nine days. Moses Titcomb wrote letters home to his brother, telling him how many ships and supplies they had captured and asking after his wife and children. When the fort surrendered, Titcomb's company of Newbury farm boys was celebrated as "proving the most destructive to the fortress." The Newbury men stayed behind to guard the town after its surrender, but they quickly became anxious to return home. Titcomb wrote to his brother, "The soldiers grow uneasy on account of their being here so long; but more especially for fear they shall be forced to stay here all winter."

After a few more months in Louisburg, Titcomb was put in charge of the forces stationed in Portland, Maine, and his company returned home. He was a very popular war hero in the colony and a celebrated hometown boy in Newbury.

Portrait of Moses Titcomb. *Courtesy of the Newburyport Public Library.*

Wolfe Tavern was opened in 1762 by William Davenport at the corner of State Street and Threadneedle Alley. It would serve the people of Newburyport for nearly two centuries. *Courtesy of the Historical Society of Old Newbury.*

Another area of French control formed the boundary between the English and French colonies in America along Lake George and the St. Lawrence River. A decade after his expedition to Louisburg, Moses Titcomb was a colonel in charge of the Essex County regiment, and he joined an expedition to Crown Point, a substantial French fortification in the Champlain Valley. Before Titcomb's departure, Reverend John Lowell, minister of the Market Square third parish meetinghouse, preached a send-off sermon to Titcomb and his regiment, in which he wished for the company

> *that you may recover our rights, that you may again humble those who have encroached upon them, even those French to whom you with other brave New England men have proved superior; that you may be saved in all dangers and all those with you, through God's gracious presence and care, and (by the will of God) be returned to us with joy, being crowned with victory.*[97]

Four months later, Moses Titcomb was dead, shot through the side by an Indian fighting with the French. There were great outpourings of grief in Newbury at the death of Colonel Titcomb. He was the grandson of one of Newbury's first settlers, and

The last incarnation of Wolfe Tavern, at the corner of Harris and State Street. It was demolished in 1953. *Courtesy of the Historical Society of Old Newbury.*

his extended family was involved in every aspect of Newbury life (he himself had nine children, eight of whom lived to adulthood). Memorial services were held in Market Square, and several pamphlets were published praising him as a hero and an example to others.

Newbury men continued to fight at Crown Point for another four years. Newbury men also accompanied the British officer General James Wolfe, who finally took Quebec City in 1759, signaling the end to major French power in North America. General Wolfe was killed in the attempt, but his victory was celebrated in Market Square with an ox roast, speeches and music. The ultimate compliment was paid to him by the townsfolk, who named their tavern after him in 1762. Wolfe Tavern, with its large sign inviting patrons to have a drink "where your ancestors tarried," remained a fixture in downtown Newburyport until it was torn down in 1953.

CHAPTER 23

THE END OF AN ERA

1764 and After

Whereas the town of Newbury is very large, and the inhabitants of that part of it, who dwell by the water side there, as it is commonly called, are mostly merchants, traders and artificers, and the inhabitants of the other part of the town are chiefly husbandmen, by means whereof many difficulties and disputes have arisen in managing their public affairs.[98]
—*Newburyport Act of Incorporation, 1764*

By 1760, power and wealth in Newbury was becoming increasingly concentrated near the bustling waterfront. In 1744, a new prison and workhouse had been built on Federal Street. In 1748, a long, narrow building was erected next to Frog Pond (now Bartlett Mall), where rope fibers were laid out and twisted, another sign of the increasing maritime trade. The port had its own schools, it was already its own parish and in 1762, wealthy merchants raised enough money to build a courthouse on the corner of Essex and State Street, against the wishes of the rest of the town. In 1761, wealthy merchant Michael Dalton imported a fire engine from London to serve the needs of the waterside.

With all that the port residents had been able to achieve themselves, they found that Newbury residents living as far away as the Bradford line or the Parker River were unlikely to vote to provide funds for schools, fire protection or waterfront improvements. When the town refused to allow court to be held in the building they had just paid to erect, it was the last straw. In June 1763, 206 men sent a petition to the General Court, listing their issues with the rest of Newbury and asking that they be set off as a separate town. The petition emphasized the growing disparity of interests between the merchants, traders and mechanics of the port and the husbandmen and farmers of the rest of Newbury.

The General Court heard the town's objections to the loss of the greatest part of its tax base, but it was not convinced. On January 28, 1764, the General Court carved Newburyport out of the vast acreage of Newbury, ordering that the area from Bromfield Street to Oakland Street be set off and incorporated as a new town. The Court agreed with the petitioners that

> *the town of Newbury is very large, and the inhabitants of that part of it, who dwell by the water side there, as it is commonly called, are mostly merchants, traders and artificers,*

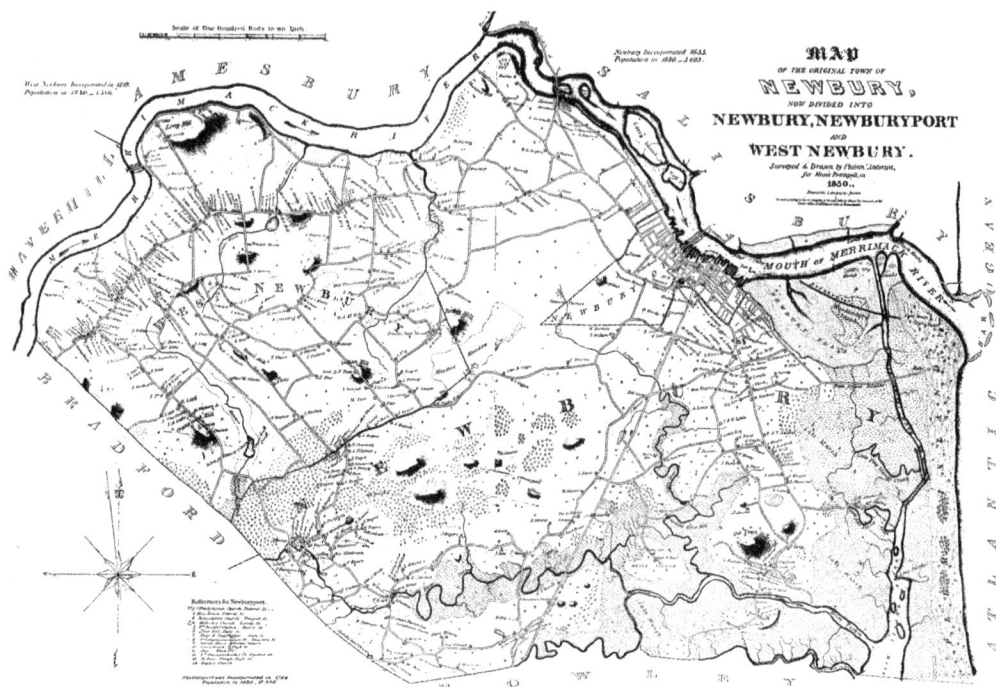

Newbury in 1850. Settlement patterns begun in the seventeenth century continued. Note the houses clustered around the waterfront and along the Bradford Road. *Private collection.*

and the inhabitants of the other part of the town are chiefly husbandmen, by means whereof many difficulties and disputes have arisen in managing their public affairs.[99]

The new town of Newburyport was granted one representative, the same as was allowed for the whole remainder of Newbury. Though there were still disputes about public buildings paid for by all the inhabitants of Newbury that took longer to resolve, the General Court's decision signaled the death of Old Newbury and the birth of a port city with a major role to play in the war for colonial independence that was right around the corner. It was in Wolfe Tavern in 1765 that the men of Newburyport, whose mercantile interests were so aligned with those of the British, first took up the challenge of resisting the Stamp Act (and rang up quite a liquor bill in the process). Newbury would continue to shrink over the centuries. In 1819, West Newbury would split off, and Belleville, in the west end of present-day Newburyport (roughly coterminous with the Plains), was briefly set off as a separate town in 1829 and then annexed to Newburyport, along with Joppa Flats and part of Plum Island, in 1851.

Though the urban merchants and seamen whose interests spurred the birth of Newburyport were very different from the Puritan cattlemen who first settled Newbury, they would have recognized in each other the same enterprising spirit. Just as the settlers had taken on the wilderness and joined the fight against the French and their allies, so too would Newburyport's sons leave by the hundreds to fight the British. The mercantile

Rear view of Thurlow House, built circa 1725 and torn down to build Route 1 cutoff. This was a typical Newbury dwelling of the time, with a saltbox roofline and rear chimneys. *HABS photograph.*

Clam huts on Joppa. *Courtesy of the Historical Society of Old Newbury.*

Skiffs on the salt marsh. Photograph by George E. Noyes. *Courtesy of Historic New England.*

pursuits that had driven settlers to first put to sea would see Newburyport the queen of the sleek clipper ships that dominated trade in the early nineteenth century. The same religious tension that caused so much disorder among the Puritans would prick the conscience of later Newburyport men and women, who followed hometown boy William Lloyd Garrison into the abolitionist fray. And in amongst the great scandals, debates and conflicts that rocked the community, there were ordinary men, women and children whose stories were told on their tombstones, in the court records and in scraps of memory handed down through generations. It is there, at the intersection between great events and ordinary lives, that a town lives, carrying the marks of its people in fields and walls and houses.

NOTES

CHAPTER 1

1. Hodge, *Handbook of American Indians*, 41.
2. Townsend, *Sand Dunes and Salt Marshes*, 224.
3. Winthrop, *Winthrop's Journal*, 69.

CHAPTER 3

4. Mather, *Magnalia Christi Americana*, 482.
5. Coffin, *Sketch of the History of Newbury*, 166. Hereafter Coffin.
6. Currier, *History of Newbury, Mass.*, 651. Hereafter Currier, *History*.

CHAPTER 4

7. Coffin, 19.
8. Currier, *History*, 92.
9. Dow, *History of the Town of Hampton*, 70.
10. Currier, *"Ould Newbury"*, 315.

CHAPTER 5

11. Currier, *History*, 57.
12. Wood, *New England's Prospect*, 101.
13. Currier, *History*, 501.

CHAPTER 6

14. Currier, *History*, 22.
15. Ibid., 413.

CHAPTER 7

16. Currier, *History*, 82.
17. *Proprietors' Book*, Vol. 1, folio 44.
18. Coffin, 44–46; Currier, *History*, 87.

CHAPTER 8

19. Currier, *"Ould Newbury"*, 94.

CHAPTER 9

20. *Records and Files of the Quarterly Courts* 4, 140. Hereafter *Quarterly Courts.*
21. Currier, *"Ould Newbury"*, 61.
22. Coffin, 54.
23. *Quarterly Courts* 1, 220.
24. *Quarterly Courts* 4, 136.
25. Coffin, 58.
26. *Quarterly Courts* 1, 200.
27. Ibid., 419.
28. Coffin, 58.
29. Currier, *History*, 163.
30. Coffin, 60.
31. *Quarterly Courts* 4, 245.
32. Currier, *History*, 158.

CHAPTER 10

33. *Quarterly Courts* 2, 219.
34. Ibid., 103.
35. Macy, *Genealogy of the Macy Family*, 21.
36. *Quarterly Courts* 2, 161.
37. Ibid., 219.
38. Emery, *Reminiscences of a Nonagenarian*, 142.
39. Bishop, *New England Judged*, 400.

CHAPTER 11

40. *Quarterly Courts* 3, 54–55.
41. Ibid., 47–50.
42. Bishop, *New England Judged*, 239–40.
43. Coffin, 69.
44. Ibid., 71.
45. *Quarterly Courts* 3, 194.

CHAPTER 12

46. Coffin, 74.
47. Noyes and Noyes, *Genealogical Record*, 29.
48. Coffin, 74.
49. Ibid., 75.
50. Except where noted, the quotations in this section come from Coffin, 82–85.
51. *Quarterly Courts* 4, 360.
52. Coffin, 101.
53. Mather, *Magnalia Christi Americana*, 486.

CHAPTER 13

54. *Probate Records of Essex County* 3, 57.
55. Mather, *Magnalia Christi Americana*, 486.

CHAPTER 14
56. Coffin, 124.
57. Hall, *Witch-Hunting*, 239.

CHAPTER 15
58. Coffin, 122.
59. See note 47.
60. Coffin, 146.
61. Currier, *History*, 155.
62. Ibid., 244.

CHAPTER 16
63. Coffin, 150.
64. Ibid.
65. Currier, *History*, 196.
66. Coffin, 159.

CHAPTER 17
67. Coffin, 161–62.
68. Coffin, 154.
69. See note 55.
70. Coffin, 162.

CHAPTER 18
71. Coffin, 168.
72. Currier, *History*, 335.
73. Rogers et al., *Death the Certain Wages of Sin*, 97.
74. Collections of the Massachusetts Historical Society, 345–46.

CHAPTER 19
75. 1924 edition, 126–27.
76. Parkman, *Half-century of Conflict*, 45.
77. Currier, *History*, 523.
78. Ibid., 533.
79. See epigraph.
80. Coffin, 172.

CHAPTER 20
81. Coffin, 177.
82. Ibid., 179
83. Ibid.
84. Coffin, 180.
85. Ibid., 182.
86. Ibid.
87. Addison, *Life and Times of Edward Bass*, 40; Coffin, 183.
88. Addison, *Life and Times of Edward Bass*, 39.

CHAPTER 21

89. Coffin, 211.
90. Currier, *History*, 402.
91. Coffin, 199.
92. Ibid., 193.
93. Ibid., 204.
94. Ibid., 197–98.
95. Ibid., 211.
96. Currier, *"Ould Newbury"*, 529.

CHAPTER 22

97. Titcomb, *Early New England People*, 184.

CHAPTER 23

98. Coffin, 228.
99. See epigraph.

BIBLIOGRAPHY

Addison, Daniel Dulaney. *Life and Times of Edward Bass, First Bishop of Massachusetts*. Boston: Houghton Mifflin, 1897.

Bishop, George. *New England Judged by the Spirit of the Lord*. London: T. Sowle, 1702.

Cleaveland, Nehemiah. *The First Century of Dummer Academy: A Historical Discourse, Delivered at Newbury, Byfield Parish*. Boston: Nichols & Noyes, 1865.

Coffin, Joshua. *A Sketch of the History of Newbury, Newburyport, and West Newbury, from 1635 to 1845*. Boston: Samuel G. Drake, 1845.

Collections of the Massachusetts Historical Society. Vol. 1, Series 6. Boston: MHS, 1886.

Currier, John J. *History of Newbury, Mass., 1635–1902*. Boston: Damrell & Upham, 1902.

———. *"Ould Newbury": Historical and Biographical Sketches*. Boston: Damrell & Upham, 1896.

Dow, Joseph. *History of the Town of Hampton, New Hampshire: From Its Settlement in 1638 to the Autumn of 1892*. Salem, MA: Salem Press, 1894.

Emery, Sarah Anna. *Reminiscences of a Nonagenarian*. Newburyport, MA: W.H. Huse & Co., 1879.

Hall, David D., ed. *Witch-Hunting in Seventeenth-Century New England: A Documentary History, 1638–1693*. 2nd edition. Durham, NC: Duke University Press, 1999.

Historical Society of Old Newbury. *Celebration of the Two Hundred and Fiftieth Anniversary of the Settlement of Newbury*. Newburyport, MA: W.H. Huse & Co., 1885.

Hodge, Frederick Webb. *Handbook of American Indians North of Mexico*. 2 vols. Washington, DC: Government Printing Office, 1907 & 1910.

Hubbard, William. *A General History of New England: From the Discovery to MDCLXXX*. Boston: Little & Brown, 1848.

BIBLIOGRAPHY

Little, George T. *Descendants of George Little: Who Came to Newbury, Massachusetts, in 1640*. Cambridge, MA: University Press, 1877.

Macy, Silvanus Jenkins. *Genealogy of the Macy Family from 1635–1868*. Albany, NY: Munsell, 1868.

Massachusetts (Colony) County Court (Essex County). *Records and Files of the Quarterly Courts of Essex County, Massachusetts*. 9 vols. Salem, MA: Essex Institute, 1911–1975.

Massachusetts Probate Court. *The Probate Records of Essex County, Massachusetts, Vol. 3, 1675–1681*. Salem, MA: Essex Institute, 1920.

Mather, Cotton. *Magnalia Christi Americana: Or, The Ecclesiastical History of New-England*. Hartford, CT: Andrus & Son, 1855.

Newbury Proprietor Records 1637–1685. Microfiche 68. In *Massachusetts Vital Records*. Oxford, MA: Holbrook Research Institute, 2000.

Noyes, Henry E., and Harriette E. Noyes. *Genealogical Record of Some of the Noyes Descendants of James, Nicholas and Peter Noyes*. Boston: 1904.

Noyes, Horatio N. *Noyes' Genealogy: Record of a Branch of the Descendants of Rev. James Noyes*. Cleveland, OH: 1889.

Parkman, Francis. *A Half-century of Conflict: France and England in North America, Part Sixth*. Vol. 1. Boston: Little, Brown, 1920.

Perley, Sidney. *The Indian Land Titles of Essex County, Massachusetts*. Salem, MA: Essex Book and Print Club, 1912.

Philbrick, Nathaniel. *Mayflower: A Story of Courage, Community, and War*. New York: Viking, 2006.

Rogers, John, Nicholas Noyes, William Hubbard, Joseph Gerrish, Esther Rodgers, et al. *Death the Certain Wages of Sin to the Impenitent: Life the Sure Reward of Grace to the Penitent*. 1701.

Titcomb, Sarah Elizabeth. *Early New England People: Some Account of the Ellis, Pemberton, Willard, Prescott, Titcomb, Sewall and Longfellow, and Allied Families*. Boston: W.B. Clarke & Carruth, 1882.

Townsend, Charles Wendell. *Sand Dunes and Salt Marshes*. Boston: Dana Estes & Co., 1913.

Tucker, Jonathan B. *Scourge: The Once and Future Threat of Smallpox*. New York: Grove Press, 2002.

Vital Records of Newbury, Massachusetts to the End of the Year 1849. Salem, MA: Essex Institute, 1911.

Winthrop, John. *Winthrop's Journal, "History of New England," 1630–1649*. Vol. 1. Edited by James Kendall Hosmer. New York: Charles Scribner's Sons, 1908.

Wood, William. *New England's Prospect (1634)*. Edited by Alden T. Vaughan. Amherst: University of Massachusetts Press, 1994.

INDEX

Visit us at
www.historypress.net

www.ingramcontent.com/pod-product-compliance
Lightning Source LLC
Chambersburg PA
CBHW080927100426
42812CB00007B/2392